KISS OF TAOWAY

A Father's Journey From Anxiety Towards Enlightenment

JOHN F. LEDGAR

First published by Ultimate World Publishing 2021
Copyright © 2021 John Ledgar

ISBN

Paperback: 978-1-922597-27-4
Ebook: 978-1-922597-28-1

John Ledgar has asserted his rights under the Copyright, Designs and Patents Act 1988 to be identified as the author of this work. The information in this book is based on the author's experiences and opinions. The publisher specifically disclaims responsibility for any adverse consequences which may result from use of the information contained herein. Permission to use information has been sought by the author. Any breaches will be rectified in further editions of the book.

All rights reserved. No part of this publication may be reproduced, stored in or introduced into a retrieval system, or transmitted in any form, or by any means (electronic, mechanical, photocopying, recording or otherwise) without the prior written permission of the author. Any person who does any unauthorised act in relation to this publication may be liable to criminal prosecution and civil claims for damages. Enquiries should be made through the publisher.

Cover design: Ultimate World Publishing
Layout and typesetting: Ultimate World Publishing
Editor: Alex Floyd-Douglass

Ultimate World Publishing
Diamond Creek,
Victoria Australia 3089
www.writeabook.com.au

TESTIMONIALS

"John brings to life his raw and unfiltered experiences of living through and overcoming the grip of anxiety. John's own life in reflection serves as a powerful read for anyone experiencing life's emotional rollercoaster and how spirituality can guide you through your darkest times. If you are struggling with negative thoughts or emotions, KISS of Taoway can help you take that first step to improve your quality of life, your sense of purpose and return you to your path of personal enlightenment."

Richard Hodge
Senior Manager, Government Services

"A critical look into our own thoughts and feelings on the road to discovering our self-identity."

Michael Ihle
Environmental Worker

"When we begin to explore the questions 'Who am I?' and 'Why am I here?', it usually comes from a dissatisfaction with 'What is.' Our lives are built around our experiences, they guide us and form the deep processes we use to make decisions in our lives. From a psychological perspective, this is how we shape our view of the world. When that view no longer matches how we feel inside, we experience confusion, anxieties, and self-doubt.

Introduce the concept of God or Spirituality and the foundations are literally shaken and often require us to reshape our identity and understand 'Who I Am.'.

John's telling of his story helps crystallise the importance of taking the steps to explore our experiences and what shapes our lives. In doing so, John found an inner truth and purpose that cannot be shaken or influenced by another person or situation. Having known John for some years, his willingness to explore these aspects of himself make him the perfect guide and his journey will certainly inspire others to do the same."

Matu Apiata
President Mornington Spiritualist Church, Spiritual Coach and Teacher

"I really enjoyed reading John's book. It was very courageous for him to open up as much as he did. A very personal journey about the difficulties he's faced, and I could directly connect with much of it, also."

Jason Geritz
Kindergarten Teacher

"What an inspiring and enjoyable book to read. Full of tangible titbits of workable strategies that you can utilise in your daily life."

Dianne Hume
Home Keeper

"Great book. It helped me recognise my own anxiety and how to deal with it."
Lexi Barry
Home Keeper

"Fantastic book with a very relatable subject. It changed my view of life and others around me and how to be strong and believe in myself. With inner peace and positive thoughts and prayers, humans can achieve anything. I highly recommend."
Co-written by
Eric Richmond, Conveyancer
Liz Richmond, Home Keeper
Hans Richmond, Lawyer

"John is a gentle soul with a huge desire to make a difference in the lives of others. I found his story to be so interesting, that once I started, I just had to keep reading. There are many very valuable insights woven throughout, not just for those on a similar journey to John, but for others who are facing any challenging life experience."
Christine Goritchan, Grad Dip Edn.
Medium, NLP Results Coach, Heal Your Life Facilitator and President of Seaford Spiritualist Church

DEDICATION

This book is dedicated to the people in my life who have helped to make me into the person I am today. Firstly, it is dedicated to my lovely Mum, Lavinia and my brave Father, David. You both gave me every opportunity to become the man I am.

Dad, you are no longer with us, however, I believe all the good things in me come from you. You taught me to be steadfast in my beliefs, to be honest, to stand up for myself, and to love my family.

Mum, you have always been my rock. You were the one I reached out to when my world began falling apart, and you were there without any questions.

From you both, I have learnt what is most important, and that is family and happiness. Dad, you are the inspiration for my own version of the *KISS* principle - though I prefer it as the *Keep It Simple Solution*.

KISS OF TAOWAY

To my children, Charlotte, Zoe, and Adam. When you read this book, you will see the vulnerable side of your Dad. You will also see that everyone is capable of change, and that I am a different person to who you once knew. Regardless of time and space, you are always in my heart and mind. I visit you in my dreams and we play like we did at Seaford Beach. Nothing will ever change my love for you, and if my time upon this earth were over tomorrow, I would go with a smile, knowing that one day we will be together in the *"Sweet by and by."*

Kaylene, you have been a level head for me when needed, as well as a mentor and coach. You introduced me to public speaking through *Toastmasters* and inspired me to write this book when you wrote and released your own. You also introduced me to Spiritualism many years ago, along with my Grandma, for which I am forever grateful.

Grandma, you were my first Spiritual teacher, teaching me how to meditate, and sharing some gems that have helped me understand the simplicity of what we do as Spiritualists and Mediums.

To my many teachers who I have worked with over the years, thank you for your dedication and belief in me. Miss Karen Jones from Frankston Highschool, thank you for the dedication you showed in helping me with my writing, and for giving me a much-needed boost of self-esteem at such a precarious time in my life.

To my spiritual teachers and mentors, Reverend Bob Ferguson, Boadie, Reverend Mandi Stone and Christine Goritchan, thank you. You have all played significant roles in guiding me to become the person I am.

DEDICATION

To the children, families, and colleagues I have worked with as a Kindergarten Teacher - it was a blast to be part of your lives. In your own ways, you have all inspired me and guided me to become who I am. Some of these times were very challenging, yet rewarding, whilst others were easy going and irreplaceable. Although our paths have parted, I do believe we are all better for having been a part of each other's lives.

Dianne, my love, you have been the sounding board for much of this book, as well as more things that are yet to come. I am blessed to have you in my life.

I would also like to give thanks to the Great Architect of the Universe, the great Spirit of all life, whatever you may believe that to be. It is from you that all comes, and all must return. My journey is but a speck upon the journey of all, yet may it be of guidance to those yet to walk this path.

Blessings to you all.

CONTENTS

Foreword	xiii
Chapter 1: Tao of Foundations	1
Chapter 2: Tao of Spirituality	11
Chapter 3: Tao of Reflection	23
Chapter 4: Tao of Change	37
Chapter 5: Tao of Freedom	49
Chapter 6: Tao of Learning	59
Chapter 7: Tao of Self	71
Chapter 8: Tao of Self-Honouring	81
Chapter 9: Tao of the Path	89
Chapter 10: Tao of Flow	99
Chapter 11: The KISS of Taoway	111
Tao Of Your KISS Journey	123
Thank You	127
About the Author	129
Taoway Connection	133
Connect With Me	135
Special Offers	137
Meditation Group	139
Holistic Counselling	141
Pellowah	143
Spiritual Healing	145
The "Be The Change You Want To See" Program	147

FOREWORD

The *"KISS of Taoway"* is my legacy of how I have overcome some very trying and difficult times in my life. It is a summary of stories both from the recent past, as well as from earlier in my life.

These are events that have helped to shape and mould me into the person I am today.

Through these pages, you will discover the events of my life, that have had a huge impact upon me. You will also discover the variety of ways that I have learnt to cope in an otherwise hostile environment.

It is my desire that you, the reader, will learn a lot from these stories. You will face the trials and tribulations, as I once did; and after the tests I faced, discover the lessons that I was learning.

KISS OF TAOWAY

Through deep reflection, I have been able to put together a powerful narrative from my own experiences that I trust will bear fruit for you.

As in life, the KISS of Taoway is written in the format of the tests first and the lessons you learn afterwards. Chapter Eleven is dedicated to my MVPA or *"Most Valuable Priceless Assets,"* which sum up simple principals that have helped me to understand the learning I have discovered.

Following this are sections on how you can continue your own journey, as well as connect with me to further explore yourself and your full potential.

DISCLAIMER

As this book is a summary of all my own experiences, it is necessary to disclaim that all opinions I have claimed within these pages are my own, from my own personal experience. When acting upon what you have learnt within these pages, discretion is required to ensure that what I have shared is appropriate for you and your personal circumstances.

If you have specific needs, such as mental health or other medical needs, it is important that you discuss these and what you plan to do as a result of reading this book, with an appropriately qualified professional who can meet your needs.

With this said, may you enjoy and gain insight into yourself within the pages of KISS of Taoway .

Happy reading and *"Be the change you want to see."*

Chapter 1

Tao of Foundations

I had been working as a Kindergarten Teacher for over ten years. Although I loved working with children, I was not satisfied with my career. I always felt tired, I was cranky at home, beginning to disassociate and lose myself in a mindless online game. I felt there was meant to be more to what I was doing, whilst feeling that I was not good enough at my work. Although feedback from parents and children was always positive, as was what I always received from management regarding my ability to develop relationships with families and children; I never truly felt I belonged.

At the time, I worked 40 minutes from home and had to drive both ways in peak hour traffic. Reflecting on this now, there is no wonder I was stressed. All that driving in the crazy peak hour, with everyone trying to get somewhere fast, was extremely taxing to me.

After near on 10 years of travelling all over the country for work, with several attempts at landing new positions (which I thought were going to make me happy), I was lucky enough to win a position as a Teacher at my Local Council-managed Kindergarten.

It is interesting looking back at the synchronicities that connected me to my new Kindergarten.

Firstly, the father of one of the children in the Child Care Centre I had worked at was an employee of the Local Council. He found out the day I had the interview that I had won the position - although he waited two weeks until I was informed to let me know he knew, and that he worked for them.

Secondly, in my ever-present search for a way to decrease my travel time, I would regularly drive past the Kindergarten I ended up opening as a Foundation Teacher in its first year.

Reflecting upon how the synchronicities brought me to this new position, I recall my first significant experience with synchronicity. In my early 20s, I had a significant sequence of synchronistic events that lead to a great journey of discovery.

I had returned home to study, after two years of studying in Bendigo. I had been reading James Redfield's *"The Celestine Prophecy"*. and had learnt all about synchronicity; a series of events and occurrences that are unrelated, however connected.

For several weeks or months, I had an image in my head of a horseshoe mountain range which I could not shake or place.

TAO OF FOUNDATIONS

One day, I was looking through some photos and postcards I had from my Central Oz School Camp when I was in Year 11. I came across a postcard which resembled the image I had in my head. It was a postcard of Wilpena Pound, at the beginning of the Flinders Rangers in South Australia.

I spent a couple of weeks organising and planning a solo road trip to revisit this place I once visited many years before. I planned to leave Boxing Day and drive up to Halls Gap, before heading to Wilpena Pound the next day.

I left home early on Boxing Day morning and drove all day, stopping in Ararat, before arriving at a busy Halls Gap around 5:00 pm. I drove into the caravan park and went to reception to book a campsite for one. I was really lucky, as they said they were almost booked out and usually do not hire out spaces for one. I set up my tent and decided to go for a walk before dinner.

I got back in the car and drove out of the caravan park, heading left. I saw a sign pointing to Halls Gap scenic lookout, so I pulled over and began up the track. After passing a few people with a casual *"Hello"* here and there, I stopped at a look out.

It was a nice view, but the track continued, and I felt as if I needed to follow where it went. I walked for another 10 or so minutes in the serenity and peace of the bush before I noticed the track was beginning to look less and less travelled. Eventually, I came to a fork in the track. It branched off in two directions.

One direction looked relatively new, although overgrown on the track and disappeared around a slight bend only about 10 metres in that direction. The second path appeared more travelled, however had a branch across it at around chest height.

KISS OF TAOWAY

I decided to follow the second track, as it seemed to stand out more, which I took as a sign it was the right choice.

A little further up the track I began to hear cars and shortly came to a road. On the other side of the road, I could see the path was blocked, or - should I say replaced - by large boulders. I crossed the road and stood looking at the boulders, contemplating my next course of action. I looked down the hill where it looked like a path cut across the bottom of the boulders; and I looked up the hill where it became quite dense, and I would have to follow the road. Eventually, I looked back at the boulders and noticed a small bird, possibly a female Fairy Wren, sitting on the boulders. As I looked at it a little closer, it skipped a little further away from me.

I continued to consider my options, and when I returned to look at the boulders and the little bird, it skipped away again. I thought to myself that this was a sign to follow the bird and as I stepped onto the boulders, the bird skipped a little further away with each step I took; as if guiding me safely across these boulders.

After 10 or 20 metres, I reached solid ground on the other side and found the continuation of the path. I followed the path and the bird, as it flitted from branch to branch and tree to tree. As I turned a bend in the path and I saw a car in the parking area, the little bird flew away.

Not sure where to go, I walked up to the car and asked the young couple in it, where Halls Gap was. They proceed to inform me that Halls Gap was the town we could see in the valley below us. They also pointed out *"The Elephant's Hide"*, which was a large rocky formation in the Grampians and quite a challenging climb - no, I didn't climb it!

TAO OF FOUNDATIONS

Shortly after a quick period of discussion, the couple offered me a lift back down the road to my car. After an eventful day, I retired for a restless night in a busy caravan park.

Waking early the next morning, I prepared for the next leg of my trip. This was uneventful until I needed to stop and get petrol just north of Adelaide. After paying for the petrol, I went back to car and discovered it would not start. This was not uncommon, and I knew how to rectify the problem. I went inside the service station again and asked the attendant to help me push the car out of the lane so that others could still fill up, then I went to work attempting to start my car. I grabbed my trusty screwdriver and tapped the starter motor repeatedly, then jumped back in the car.

Tick. Tick. Tick. That is all I heard as I turned the key. The starter motor had seized up.

I continued to work on the starter motor. Tap, tap, tap. Tick, tick, tick.

Eventually, after about 10 minutes or so, a young man walked past. I think he was in his mid-20s. He asked if I needed some help and I, of course, said yes. He said he would help me in exchange for a lift up the road. And just like that, just as I was beginning to think I would have to call the RACV, help had come along.

Within a few minutes we were back on the road. We chatted whist I drove, and I eventually dropped him off to continue our journeys separately.

That night, I stayed at Mount Remarkable, halfway between Adelaide and Port Augusta. A nice little camping site that is very much based on an honesty system of paying a few dollars into a box and filling in your car rego on a slip you leave on your windscreen.

A more restful night saw me rise early the next morning and set off again towards Wilpena Pound. I stopped in Port Augusta and bought two new tyres as my re-treads were beginning to go bald. Whilst I was waiting for my car to get ready, a gentleman of around 30 years of age or so was dropped off with a flat tyre.

We began to chat, and he told me he was heading to Melbourne to visit his relatives when he got his flat tyre and had to get a lift, leaving his wife and kids on the side of the road, just north of Port Augusta. As I explained I was heading towards Wilpena Pound, he gave me directions, and I offered to give him a lift back out to his car. He gratefully accepted.

After dropping him off and saying our farewells, I headed back into Port Augusta and out towards Wilpena Pound. After two and a half days, I arrived at Wilpena Pound. I was excited to be there, but it was not as I remembered. I was parked outside the Pound, and had to walk in. I walked about halfway up one of the slopes before turning around, exhausted, and longing to be home (as you do when you are far from home on a journey). I took some photos and began the return trip to the car.

Lo and behold, when I turned the key in the ignition the car would not start again. This time, I was able to enlist the assistance of some foreign tourists who were passing by as I needed help. With their assistance, I got the car started again and was on my return trip home. What took me nearly three days to complete on the outward journey, only took little over 24 hours on the way home. By the time I was returning, I had lost the feeling of excitement, of being in a flow state. From memory, nothing really interesting occurred on the return trip.

I realise that during this whole journey of discovery, I was focusing very much inwardly, whilst keeping an outward focus. A paradox I would have to navigate for many years until I learned its lesson.

I wonder how my life would have turned out if I could have kept that inward focus from that time on. On both these occasions, the journey of discovery I took going to Wilpena Pound and landing my current role as a Kindergarten Teacher, I had been able to tap into the abundant potential that is synchronicity. In both situations, I had aligned many things in my life, so that I was working in accordance with my highest good. The downside is, that I was not able to maintain this connection.

Why you may ask? I believe the reason why I, like so many other people are not able to reach their potential for happiness, abundance, and success, is because I was looking for it in the wrong place.

On my journey to Wilpena Pound, I was focused on where I was going, rather than the journey itself.

It is not the outcome that is important, but the process.

This is an important piece of learning I have achieved through being a Kindergarten Teacher. When a child paints a picture or builds a castle; we praise the outcome: *"Great painting!"* or *"That's an awesome tower!"*

This is the response we often give and receive. What we need to focus on instead, is the process of *how* we were able to achieve something.

This often has nothing to do with the external finished product, but rather, more to do with the internal learning that has gone on. Acknowledging the effort, process and thought we put into things - whether we are a child or an adult - is more important than the finished product. What I missed during my trip to Wilpena Pound was the potential meditative and internal dialogue with myself, which I was totally unaware of, such as my fears, passions and even values. That I am enough, whether I made it to Wilpena Pound or not.

By focusing on the process, we are more readily able to bring ourselves into the present moment, which is where all the magic of life occurs.

With regards to landing my current position and the synchronicity I could have tapped into; well, I should say I started off in my own power. Full of confidence in my own abilities again after so much doubt. However, again, I did not internalise this belief in myself. Eventually, I would discover that I was doing a lot of people-pleasing behaviours, which I think I also displayed in my interview. Rather than being honest with myself, I did what I felt I had to, to keep my job and develop my skills.

It was around this time that I was formally diagnosed as suffering from Generalised Anxiety Disorder. If only I had listened to myself - my true self - I would have discovered that by reflecting upon myself and going inward, I would have a greater understanding of who I was and what I am here to do.

TAO OF FOUNDATIONS

My biggest takeaway from this experience, is that I can tap into the synchronicities that surround me and gain from the abundance that the Universe has in store for me.

However, it starts with me first.

That is, by going inside and reflecting on past behaviours and situations I have been through and how I have responded or reacted to them. Once I began to accept my own responsibility and make internal shifts towards the person I wanted to be, I began to notice that I was happier, and I was living more aligned to my values and thus, beginning to develop a clearer picture of my purpose.

The biggest thing I can share with you right now, is regardless of what is happening in your life, ask yourself, *"What am I learning from this?"*

This is not the be-all and end-all of how to live a happier life. However, it is a question that has helped me through some of the most trying times of my life to date.

When you begin to ask yourself, *"What am I learning from this?"*, you will be amazed at the things you will discover about yourself. You will discover what sort of mindset you have. You will learn if you are prejudiced or biased in certain ways. By asking yourself to examine your circumstances truthfully, you are inviting yourself to grow and evolve on a more conscious level.

Chapter 2

Tao of Spirituality

For as long as I can remember, I have always believed in some sort of higher spiritual purpose to life. I have not always practiced or stayed true to myself, however, and have strayed from my path on more than one occasion.

In my opinion, holding on to your own personal spiritual beliefs is essential to living a happy and productive life. When I discuss spirituality, I do not refer to religion as such, because I know that not everyone believes or follows a religion.

However, I believe everyone can be spiritual in their own way.

I remember learning from a History Unit when I was studying my Bachelor of Arts at Monash University. I was taught that all religions were written by man, and as such, are man's interpretation of that which they cannot know. This really impacted on my perspective of religious text and as an extension, religion as a whole.

On the other hand, it strengthened my perspective of spirituality, which I believe is to do with how we treat ourselves and others around us.

My earliest memory of religion is that if you are bad, you go to Hell. That is all I remember from Sunday School, which I believe I attended twice before refusing and spending a service with Mum and Dad in the main service.

To the best of my recollection, my family stopped attending church shortly after this. This is also the belief I gained from my R.E. class in Primary School. While I believe that there is no problem teaching children about spirituality, I do believe that religion should be kept until one is old enough to make a sound decision on which to learn. Otherwise, it is indoctrination, and history has shown us all how harmful this can be.

I remember some of my friends talking about God and their faith. Most I would assume were either Catholic or Christian of some denomination. One day, as they were talking, I remember saying, *"Well, my God is stronger than yours. He comes from another planet. That's why he is stronger."*

Although I cannot remember the exact reason why I said this, I believe it is because I believed in a good God, a kind God who protects and helps you; not a punitive God as many Christians are taught about, who will punish you for being *"bad."* I also remember thinking this concept of sin, particularly original sin that we inherit just through being born, was illogical and not worthy of my time.

As I grew older, I developed an interest in spirituality but was unaware of exactly what it was. Once, in my late teens or early twenties, two or three people, who were Jehovah Witnesses, came to the house and began to give their little speech. Although I found some of what they were saying interesting, I refused to buy into their belief system. It was wrong for me.

Alternatively, I began to tell them that what I believed in was *"Something like the force from Star Wars."*

In some ways I still do, realising that we are all made up of various forms of energy that is solidified into a physical form. Furthermore, I believe that an aspect of this energy survives what we know as death and moves to another level of existence.

Many texts I have read recently and in the not-so-distant past, talk of a God of love, or a God force within. Some even refer to God as the Universe. In these versions, I see a belief in a supreme being or even a collected energy of growth and advancement which we can all tap into.

Later still, I began to read lots about the paranormal, including a book on the predictions of Nostradamus. This really inspired me significantly, as I had had some rather interesting experiences and vivid predictive dreams in my childhood and early to mid-teens.

It has come to my attention over the years, that the punitive God that we learn about in the Bible and other religious text of that era, is how man understood God at the time. That it is also the God they required to assist them to build societies that do not require an angry God to rule over them. Thus, I believe that the concept of *"God"* is gradually changing with the evolution of mankind.

One of these experiences had me wide awake in my room one night. I cannot remember how old I was, but I am thinking around 10 years of age. I recall my Dad, or who I thought was my Dad, walk into my room, pass the foot of the bed, and look out my bedroom window by pulling back the curtain a little bit. I did not see him return.

The next morning, I asked Dad if he came into my bedroom that night and he said he did not. I was at a loss and still am as to who it was.

Another time, around 15 years old, I had been playing as part of my Dad's cricket team. That Saturday night, after fielding all day, I went to sleep and had a very vivid and - as it turned out - very predictive dream.

In my dream, my Uncle Ernie was going out to bat. I watch him grab his bat, put it under his arm and walk out on to the field. He faced a few balls. Suddenly, he swung at a ball going down the legside and the keeper caught the ball. There was a huge appeal, and the umpire gave him out.

The next day, we were batting. It should have been a cinch; however, we began losing a lot of wickets. Then it came time for Ernie to go out and bat. I had seen him bat many times that season. Something in the way of the events of the present moment made me want to shout out to Ernie, *"Watch your legside!"*

But I couldn't.

TAO OF SPIRITUALITY

As Ernie batted, I was mesmerised by how familiar the scene in front of me was and that I could do nothing to prevent what I knew was going to happen. A few balls later, I watched as Ernie swung at a ball down the legside and was given out caught behind. I was devastated because I believed I could have prevented this.

Could I? I will never know.

This was the second time, that I had had a predictive dream. The first time was several years earlier, when I was in Primary School. I dreamt that I was walking home from school, and this girl was there. I knew I recognised her; however, I could not recall her. I remembered a girl we had played Newcomb against in school, who looked similar, but realised it was not her. Two days later, I met my sister's friend, Jodie.

It was her I had met, before I met her.

As the years passed, I still held onto a belief in something greater. I was fascinated with the supernatural and paranormal. I explored séances with friends, not realising that we were potentially putting ourselves at risk. We were untrained and not using protection of any sort.

Luckily, no one was hurt by this, however, we did receive quite a scare once when a spirit said they used to play practical jokes and began spelling out *"B-L-U-,"* at which time we had quickly removed our hands from the glass, assuming it was *"blood"* they were spelling out. My friend Doug found his dog with a cut on his foot.

Needless to say, that was the last time we played around with that.

KISS OF TAOWAY

During my mid-to-late teens, my experiences began to decrease, although I was still fascinated with the supernatural and paranormal. In Year 11, I was studying Psychology. My teacher, Miss Jones, was teaching us meditation and we were practising a body relaxation technique. I remember relaxing all the way from the feet, up my legs, torso, and arms; however, once she began to talk us through relaxing our face and head, I was suddenly somewhere else. I remember being on a beach, with cliffs nearby.

It felt familiar. It was really vivid. The teacher was there and there were tents and a bonfire. I remember speaking to someone and then suddenly, the school bell went, and I was jolted back to the present.

This fascinated me.

The power of the mind to be able to bring such relaxation, as well as other possibilities in this altered state. Knowing my Grandma, (my Mum's Mum), was spiritual and practised meditation, as well as running these things called *"Circles."*

I asked Grandma to teach me to meditate. She made me a simple meditation cassette, - yes, we had cassettes back then! -with a visualisation that would assist me to learn to meditate.

Each night, I would lie down and listen to this meditation to help me relax and eventually fall asleep. It went something like this:

"Picture yourself on a small boat. The boat is floating on a lake. Lay down and focus on your breath. Feel the water rock the boat…"

I always pictured myself lying down on this little wooden boat, in the middle of a still and peaceful lake, surrounded by trees and mountains, the blue sky and a few clouds above me. I continued for many years, using this meditation cassette, even when I moved away from home to go to university.

It wasn't until I returned home from University in my early 20s, that I would begin to go to the Mornington Spiritualist Church with my sister and Grandma, and then later to Seaford Church and Dromana Church. I always loved going along, meditating, and occasionally receiving a reading during their *"Proof of Survival"* demonstration.

Unfortunately, as many young people do, I had been experimenting with marijuana. Although I loved the feeling at the time, I am so grateful that it is no longer a part of my life.

Many times, I would turn up to Mornington Spiritualist Church, having spent the week smoking, to be approached by the Reverend Bob Ferguson. He would usually address me with a smile – and then a frown - like this, *"Hi John, I know what you've been doing. Get up there and do some healing."*

And so, this began my initiation into spiritual healing. This concept of the *"laying on of hands"* was one that would become quite familiar to me, as I would develop my spiritual healing medium skills over the next several years.

I cannot remember exactly when, but sometime after attending the Mornington Spiritualist Church, I began to look for a development circle to join. After working with a few teachers and changes in my working status, I began sitting with my first teacher, Boadie.

We would sit once a week and focus a lot on meditation, how we felt, and what we experienced during the meditations. I would also receive spiritual healing from Boadie regularly for some time. I always felt great after an energy healing from her. Eventually my work status changed again and I had to find yet another teacher.

This time, I would join Reverend Mandi Stone of the Berwick Spiritualist Church. I would continue to sit with Mandi for the next five to six years, developing my healing, mediumship skills, trans-meditation channelling, as well as learning Tarot and level one Reiki with a Reiki Master.

During this time, I would regularly read books on Spiritual Development, as well as discuss with Mandi and the other students, my sister and eventually my partner of the time, about different things related to spirituality, the continuation of the soul beyond the veil of death, and deeper aspects of life.

I was growing in confidence in my ability to work with spirituality and use this to help people. At the same time, I was growing increasingly dissatisfied with my career.

Unfortunately, as I still had not learnt that happiness comes from within, I was still looking outwardly for things to make me happy. I no longer smoked marijuana, I only drank moderately and on special occasions, but I was developing an unhealthy obsession with games on my iPhone and becoming increasingly stressed, due to my lack of confidence in my ability at work.

I would eventually reduce meditating as regularly as I had and became more focused on my career. I began to look into personal training and decided that I would stop attending the development circle that was a saving grace in a dark time; so that I could put the money away and save for the training of my new career.

TAO OF SPIRITUALITY

This, however, did not go to plan.

I awoke one morning with pain in my chest. Every time I breathed in, it hurt. I rang work and said I would not be in and got a lift to the GP. The doctor immediately put me on an ECG machine and afterwards sent me to Casey Hospital with a letter.

After being taken into the emergency department, given some angina medication, having my blood taken and some scans, I was released with some follow-up test plans. Eventually, I discovered that the cause of the pain was deep bruising from a minor car accident that had happened several weeks earlier and had not manifested itself until that day.

This whole ordeal put an immediate stop to my personal training plans.

I continued working in my job, dissatisfied and longing for something to make me happy. Eventually, I enrolled in an open learning course and undertook a Graduate Diploma of Primary Education, to add to my Early Childhood Education qualification, which opened up my opportunities to change positions. Receiving high grades and an offer to apply for a course in Honours or a Master of Education, I thought I was on the right path. I loved learning to teach Primary School-aged children. However, I still felt conflicted, as I knew that if I did get a job as a teacher, it would be up to me to teach the way I had been taught in my course - not the way I had learned that students are still taught.

The system of teaching I learned, was quite similar to how we teach in early childhood at kindergartens and childcare centres; individually focused, based on the child's strengths and interests.

However, whilst on my placements I noticed teachers were finding it very challenging to be able to undertake this style of teaching, whilst at the same time sticking to the prescribed curriculum.

This time of learning was significant for me, even though I strayed from my spiritual path for a while. It taught me that true happiness does not come from an external place or thing.

Happiness found in this way is fleeting.

As I would discover, within a couple of years when I landed my next new position at a local council in a Sessional Kindergarten. I found a small increase in satisfaction; however, the stress did not go away. In fact, I was diagnosed with anxiety which sent me spiralling - much like Alice - down the rabbit whole of despair.

Why didn't this new role - which was something I had dreamt about for years - bring me satisfaction? The only answer I could come up with, is that it did not come from within. Deep inside, I knew that I was good at working with children, however this was not where my passion was.

It was my connection with my true self that would eventually guide me towards my own happiness.

Working with several Counsellors over many years, I began to realise that it was my mindset that I needed to focus on. However, as I spent time going to Counsellor after Counsellor and telling them my story, it became apparent it was down to me to put in the hard work. I was close to giving up on counselling, as none of them gave me any strategies to work with or things to work on to shift my anxiety. That was until I met my last

Counsellor, Bronwyn, who on the first meeting asked me what I wanted and how I felt the sessions would go. We discussed developing strategies and within a few weeks, I was noticing changes happening within myself.

Ultimately what I learned, is that spirituality truly is an internal journey. You can go to as many self-help gurus and Counsellors as you want, but the path to spiritual fulfilment comes when you focus on going internally and focusing on your true self and what you can learn from you, *about you*. This, however, is not an easy thing to do.

Sometimes it means we must look at the darkness within us, to be able to discover our light.

For me, I have discovered that going internally and embracing the darkness within has helped me to accept I am human and will make mistakes. It has also helped me to understand that there is always opportunity for redemption. Though spirituality and mental health are two very different concepts, for me I have discovered that by truly embracing who I am as a spiritual being, not only have I increased my sense of spiritual connections, but also has the positive side effect of managing my anxiety and the symptoms I experienced better, as you are guided to live in line with your true self and your values. I believe that the ancient masters of Tibet, China and even the Americas understood this concept in some way.

When we look at the human body, a plant, or even a rock, we are looking at a whole that is created by collective a unification of the microverse that makes it up. I am talking specifically about cells, atoms and neutrons. They are the microverse that make up the whole of everything we see, hear and experience.

KISS OF TAOWAY

When you look at these unseen things, through powerful microscopes, we begin to see similarities between everything. Using specialist imaging equipment, scientists can measure energy that is created at this micro level.

As everything in our known universe is made up of atoms, does it not follow that everything is made up of energy, vibrating at different levels? If we are made up of energy, and even our thoughts and words can be measured energetically, then should we not be able to tap further and further into this knowledge with every generation?

Do not accept my words, for they are my understanding of how spirituality and the universe works. Instead, use my words as a guide to direct you forward in your own learning and understanding of your own spirituality - and the universe as a whole.

Chapter 3

Tao of Reflection

We all need someone that we trust, who we can divulge our deepest secrets and yearnings, from time to time. Most of the time, this person can be a friend, lover, or colleague; almost anyone you are confident to speak to and share your thoughts and dreams with.

Sometimes, we need that person to be more specialized and trained, such as a Doctor, Counsellor or Psychologist.

When life begins to weigh you down and you start to feel as if you are crumbling under the pressure and stress of your day-to-day life, then it is time for you to find that professional. Someone trained to help you understand where you have diverted from your truth.

KISS OF TAOWAY

Having spent many hours myself in the office of a Counsellor, I know the importance of finding the right fit for you.

My first experience of counselling came when I was studying my Bachelor of Arts at La Trobe University, Bendigo. My sister helped me get some counselling after having a huge bender at a mate's 21st Birthday.

After attempting to give a speech for my friend on the occasion of his 21'st birthday and being rudely interrupted several times by another friend who kept distracting me, I called out, *"Let's all get drunk!"*

I proceeded, true to my words, and got so drunk; I do not remember much of the night. I do remember headbutting one poor fella and later trying to get up off the ground. I had been punched out for being a jerk and the bloke who hit me was standing over me, telling me not to get up.

Later on, I found out that my sister had almost ran me over in her car as I was walking home after that party. This scenario raised real concerns for my family and me. Shortly after, I began my on-off relationship with counselling.

I cannot remember the first session with a Counsellor, but I do remember when I returned to Bendigo, I got in touch with the student welfare people and began weekly counselling for months. I remember I would talk about how I was always overwhelmed and found it hard to express my emotions.

I cannot remember much of my experience back then. It helped a little bit, yet in hindsight, it really felt like it was like putting a tiny band aid over a huge gash. It never really helped me to cope with or develop skills to manage the way I felt or express my feelings.

Many years down the track, I again felt overwhelmed and stressed all the time and was referred to a Psychologist for counselling. This was through my local GP and to be honest, I eventually removed myself from his service as we discussed something different each week. However, I never received any guidance in strategies or suggestions on how to cope; other than, *"If driving so far for work is causing you stress, why don't you get a job closer to home?"*

This, I felt at this time, was not practical or ever possible having applied for several positions closer to home and getting knocked back every time.

After several years of persisting, things came to a head again. I remember the exact event. It was the second Wednesday of the first term school holidays in 2013. I had been watching the kids all day whilst my wife was at work. The in-laws had come over a little bit later in the afternoon.

I cannot remember exactly what caused my little meltdown, though.

All I remember was that our eldest wanted to go to her Nanny and Pop's house, but kept changing her mind, not wanting to leave her Mum and myself. After five or so minutes of this indecision, I said something like, *"Ok, that's it, you're not going."*

As she could not decide, I felt that no one else was making a decision, so I had to. At my announcement of this, the others decided that, in fact, *"Yes, she is going."*

KISS OF TAOWAY

I cannot remember exactly what happened after that, except that I lost it. I became really angry; ranting, and raving and storming off inside.

I felt out of control. My wife and I had a discussion and we decided that I should go and see a Counsellor to get a handle on the anger that had been creeping into me for a long time.

This time, I felt more confident with the Counsellor. In the session, he listened and near the end of the session, suggested a book for me to read: Wayne Dyer's *"Your Erroneous Zones."*

My Counsellor said that this book explains the way we create stress and anxiety in our own minds in easy-to-read language that lay people can easily understand. Within a few weeks, I had received my copy and began to read it. I regularly refer this to people I speak with, as it easily breaks down ways we self-sabotage and how we can overcome these mindsets.

The issue of medication was discussed, and my Psychologist wrote to my Doctor with recommendations for medication to help stabilise my anxiety.

Many of the issues that Dyer's book discusses I could resonate with; however, one stood out above all. That issue was people-pleasing. I did not realise it, but I had developed the self-defeating, self-sabotaging skill of being a people-pleaser. Pleasing people is fine however, it can become an issue when you are trying to please everyone. This is because it will lead you down a path where you will start to contradict yourself as you try to please everyone, as not everyone will think the same way. I also learnt that if you can get 50% of the people you talk with to agree with you, then you are doing well.

TAO OF REFLECTION

It is impossible to get everyone to agree with you.

I had two years with this Counsellor, but eventually the band aid of just talking over the issues, without unpacking them, or working on strategies to resolve or solve them became too much, and again, I was feeling out of control.

I was becoming concerned that I may be bipolar, as my mood would quickly go up and down, and I had recently learnt of a relative who had been diagnosed.

This time I went to a different GP who asked if I had seen a specialist. To this, I mentioned the counselling and he said, *"No, a Psychiatrist. For an official diagnosis."*

This led to me meeting with a Psychiatrist who confirmed that I had Generalised Anxiety Disorder, and not Bipolar Disorder. This was great. It was also fantastic how this specialist explained that in children, anxiety can be experienced as fear and it manifests in a similar way to what I was experiencing.

This Psychiatrist changed my medication and referred me to a developmental psychologist for counselling.

Generalised Anxiety Disorder, as the name describes, is a general fear or anxiety of everything. Anything can trigger you and it may appear there is no specific reason. In my opinion, it is an illogical fear, it makes no sense to me when it takes grip and can send me spiralling down the rabbit hole. My only hope is that I am able to scramble back out.

I was feeling confident that I was getting somewhere, however, I still lacked the strategies to support my anxiety. I now had the knowledge from Wayne Dyer's book, which helped somewhat. However, the occurrence of my anxiety outbursts began to increase, whilst my overall happiness was decreasing again.

My last appointment with this Counsellor, after a year and a half, was the first time any strategies were discussed with me. It was the first instance where I found that counselling was not just about me talking, but about skill development and learning strategies.

My eldest daughter was in counselling at a local service, and I was able to self-refer to this service as it was a cheaper service and much closer to home. I was also going through marriage counselling at this service, so our marriage Counsellor gave me inside information on how to do my self-referral. Within a few weeks, I had started at a new counselling service with a new Counsellor.

From this time on, everything was different. On our first appointment, Bronwyn Raffaut, a Mental Health Social Worker and Counsellor, asked me what I wanted to get out of counselling with her.

I had never been asked this question before.

I described my experience thus far, as I have shared with you above. Further to this, I said that I want to be able to learn and develop strategies to help me to manage my anxiety better, so I could feel happier, be a better husband and father.

This appointment was pivotal to my changing mindset and the growth I have experienced in the care of this Counsellor. One of the first things I remember covering with her, was my values.

TAO OF REFLECTION

Bronwyn uses ACT cards. ACT stands for Acceptance and Commitment Therapy. She spreads these cards all through the room, on the couch, the coffee table, the floor, and said for me to choose as many as I felt resonated with me. Out of the 50 or so, I think I picked up over 20, at least. This was fine she said, because I was then to pick the top 10, then out of the top 10, down to my top five. I think we got it down to three value cards eventually and unpacked them.

My top three values were family, freedom, and fun.

Family has always been important to me. Family stood out because I was in a deep period of reflection about what family meant. At this time, I was still married, though my marriage was in trouble. I was struggling with my relationship with my wife and my children. My connection with my parents and siblings was barely present, as I hardly ever contacted them.

Freedom was also very important to me.

Freedom to make choices for myself. Freedom from the consistent criticism I felt I was experiencing. Freedom to experience life as the joy it is.

Fun and making life fun was my third value. In some areas of my life, I was having lots of fun. I felt I was able to express myself as the person I was deep down, not the person I had become. I was able to be silly, adventurous, and sometimes just downright ridiculous. Making even mundane things like cleaning a painting easel or going for a walk a fun experience for myself and those around me.

KISS OF TAOWAY

Gaining an understanding of my own values helped me to begin to self-reflect and understand my values. It was also the start for the biggest shifts in my mindset further down the track.

At this time, I went to a workshop in the city on personal development and we also did an activity to discover our values and life purpose. Slowly, I realised that my values were beginning to shift.

Time passed, and I continued to work on my mindset, implementing strategies like going for walks, listening to music, and gardening. Oh, how the people of Cranbourne West must be pleased I have moved!

At that time, I would often walk to and from work, listening to music and singing at the top of my lungs, losing myself in the peace of my own voice and the music. I would also go for long walks at other times such as on the weekends, school holidays and occasionally, after work. I would often say to my colleagues and friends at the Kindergarten that I was the crazy singing man of Cranbourne West.

Time passed even more significantly, my wife and I separated and on the advice of my lawyer, I undertook a *"Men's Behaviour Change"* course. This course was a real eye-opener for me. It was quite challenging to sit through 20 weeks of 2 hours a week, listening to the facilitators refer to us as perpetrators of domestic violence. I was not the only participant who felt as if they have been labelled violent, when they felt they were not. It reminds me of another concept that Wayne Dyer's book taught me, which was to not speak in absolutes. This leads to fixed mindsets and in my opinion, is part of our overall gender and racial prejudices found throughout human society at present.

TAO OF REFLECTION

As a result of the generalisation the facilitators used, I, like many of the other participants would become argumentative at the suggestion I was a violent man. Which I am not and never will be. As I explain to the children at the Kindergartens where I teach, the same as I do to my children and grandchildren, it is ok to be angry; however, it is what you do with your anger that is important. It is never ok to hit people or hurt them in anyway; the same way it is not ok to damage things, just because you are angry.

Learning to express your anger in constructive ways is an important skill that I believe needs more focus on in all areas of education.

Although I disagree with how this particular program was run, I gained some big takeaways about myself. As time went on, I realised I needed to stop fighting them and just sit in my truth and reflect upon myself. This does not mean I stopped debating their language, as I believe that is why I was there. To help them refine how they refer to the men in the program, so they can avoid the conflict raised through labelling others in a certain way.

The biggest take away, besides learning what sort of father I wanted to be, was again, my values. As part of one of the activities, we were to choose from a list of words that represented our values. Again, we had to narrow them down to five values. This time they had some values that were not present in my previous value-exploring adventure.

This time, my top three were all connected with spirituality. This was not a surprise to me, as I had reconnected so very deeply with my spirituality after my separation; it grew during the period when my father was battling with cancer and continues to grow to this day.

KISS OF TAOWAY

I recall many sessions with my current Counsellor discussing the impact my connection to spirituality is having on my mindset. Often, I would mention things that I have been doing and she would acknowledge these as strategies for managing my anxiety and stress levels, which was particularly important at this time in my life whilst I was undergoing so many big changes. Besides the listening to music, walking, and gardening; I would often discuss the meditation I was doing, singing as part of a makeshift choir at the Seaford Spiritualist Church, experiences I was having at the development circle I attended and what I was learning from the many spiritual development books I was reading.

One thing I loved hearing from her, was her counterargument whenever I would talk about the opinion certain people had of me as a father. She would point out the growth I had shown since working with her. She would mention how I had committed to improving my parenting skills, how I had developed resilience, and various coping skills to manage the many stressors in my life. The way my mindset had changed and how I would keep check of my thoughts and ask what I was learning from this.

This brings me to one of the biggest learnings I have ever had during my time working with Counsellors. Mindset.

Our mindset has a huge bearing on our mental health.

When we move our mindset from a fixed or limiting mindset, to a growth or flexible mindset, then we can start looking at what happens in our life and what we can learn from it.

At the time of writing this, the world has been stuck in a lockdown due to the COVID-19 pandemic. What I have learnt during this time is that we can only learn from our experiences if we keep a growth mindset. During lockdown, I have been working from home, assisting with a lot of administrative duties, and developing my information technology skills such as using Excel, Word, and even expanding my understanding of Outlook.

I spent the first few weeks hammering away and completing the case studies for my Holistic Counselling course, submitting, and subsequently receiving my qualification. As well as working from home and developing my IT skills, I have also been participating in lots of training for work, for my business, as well as participating in online *Toastmasters* meetings and training.

Had I not worked on my mindset before the pandemic, I am certain I would not be managing as well as I am. They say times of trial and tribulation bring out the best and the worst in us. The worst are things we need to address ourselves and turn into a positive. The best, well they are the things people are going to remember about you. Your resilience, your compassion, your sense of humour.

Whatever it is that you have gained during times of trial and tribulation, embrace them, and share them.

My journey through counselling has helped me to understand who I am and what I value. I have received insight into my truths and what I am willing to sacrifice and what I am not. It also has taught me that sometimes you need to lose, in order to win.

As time goes on, I focus less on my mental health and more on the journey within, my values, self-focus and celebrating successes.

One thing I have mentioned to a participant in my meditation group, is that everyone has wisdom to share. We may look up to certain people for inspiration and model ourselves on the excellence we see. We may also have others who look up to us as that inspiration, as the level they wish to attain. I think this is pivotal to the human condition, particularly the future evolution.

Our unique journey brings with it a certain wisdom that is only ours.

It is our duty to share this with other people, not just for their benefit, but also for the benefit of humanity. It is only through unity can we, as a race, progress beyond the injustice and degradation that our current society has established.

The journey forward is via humility, acceptance, justice, equity, and a uniformed society that supports each other's weaknesses and lifts each other's strengths up high.

When you start to look inward, I want you to consider how you approach obstacles. Do you perceive them as the Great Wall of China, something to keep you out and prevent you from moving forward? Or is it an obstacle for you to find a way to overcome and march into your future?

When something happens that causes you stress, grievance, and pain, learn to stop.

Stop what you are doing and breathe.

Breathe in so deeply that you fill your diaphragm and then breathe out to release the stress you feel building up. Now ask yourself, *"What is this event or situation trying to teach me about myself? What am I learning from this?"*

TAO OF REFLECTION

I am not going to say that these questions are a silver bullet that will make everything right. What I am saying is that these questions will give you the opportunity to change the way you think about the situation and thus how you will respond. Notice, I said respond.

Reacting is instinctive and reflective.

Often it is done without thought about the consequences of your actions. Responding on the other hand requires that you have thought about the event or situation and made a conscious decision about how you respond.

If you have mental health concerns, please, please, please, consult with your doctor and seek professional help. Seek information from credible sources such as your pharmacist or doctor about any medication you may be prescribed, how to use it, side effects and safety information.

Also, make sure you interview your Counsellor or psychologist. Be sure that you ask them questions about their practice, how they work and what they expect of you. As well as this, be clear on your expectations. I wish I had known earlier that I could tell my Counsellor what I expected and how I wanted to work with them, such as when I told Bronwyn I wanted to develop strategies to support me to achieve my recovery goals, which firstly was to be able to manage my anxiety better, and secondly to develop better coping skills so I could be a better parent to my children, and thirdly to come off my medication.

I do understand that not everyone has the energy or the ability to articulate what they expect when they are in this space. In this situation, they may benefit from the Counsellor taking the lead and supporting them to develop that understanding, at which point, they will have greater clarity about what their expectations are.

Had I known this earlier on, I may have gotten better results with my earlier Counsellor, or I may have known to move on earlier. It is your life and your mental health, and you have a say in how you manage it.

You are the expert on being you.

I am an expert on being me.

I know how I feel, although I had to learn how to articulate my feelings effectively. Through sharing with my Counsellor and close family and friends, I have been able to develop my skills to be able to express how I feel, what emotions and why. I have also come to realise that a lot of what I feel comes from me. It is my own expectations or interpretations of what others do or say, or what I am doing and saying that creates my reality.

Remaining mindful helps me to avoid much of the stress I have created in my own life.

Chapter 4

Tao of Change

———◇◆◇◆◇———

There are certain events that have the power to totally reshape our lives.

* Star Wars Spoiler alert! * * Harry Potter Spoiler alert! *

They are epochal events like when Luke Skywalker discovers that Darth Vader is his father or when Harry Potter learns that he must die at the hand of Lord Voldermort. Not everyone has events as significant as the ones that Hollywood makes; however, everyone has them.

Starting school, making my first ton in cricket, the birth of my first child, and being installed as the Master of Berwick-Balcara

KISS OF TAOWAY

Lodge 359, on the register of the Grand Lodge of Free and Accepted Freemasons of Victoria, were all significant events that changed my life. However, these are not the only events that reshaped my life, there have been many more than I can recall.

The thing about a significant event that reshapes your life, is that it often will throw you into a totally new way of thinking about life and who you are. In my experience, the most significant event that can change the way you view life, and yourself, is through the passing of a loved one.

I was 24 years old when my Grandfather, Papa, died after a long battle with prostate cancer. This was something the family had been preparing for; for a very long time.

I had come to drop something off at Darling and Papa's house for my sister and she came out to the car to get it. She greeted me and said that Papa did not look good, and I should go home and rather remember him how I saw him last time.

It was not until my own father died that I understood why she protected me and my memory, and I am forever grateful for that.

I received a call a little later that day, saying he had died, and I quickly returned to my Grandparent's house to start grieving with the rest of the family. It is quite a blur, looking back on this 21 years later.

Papa was a gentle man and respected and loved by all who knew him.

Things did change; we grieved and moved on with life.

TAO OF CHANGE

I still recall Papa's last words to me. I had called in to visit him and Darling after cricket, and as I was saying goodbye after our chat, he said *"Don't make too many runs."*

I never spoke to him again.

Since I often find hidden significance in things that happen around or to me, I have often wondered what was meant here. I like to think that Papa was pointing out that there was more to life than cricket and that I must not put all my focus on one thing. Then again, he may have just been acknowledging the ton I had made and that it is good to let others have their successes.

I still remember that weekend.

It was such a long and sad one. Not only did we have to prepare Papa's funeral, but we also had to prepare to support Papa's best friend, Harold, as he farewelled his wife, Normie. I had never felt this sort of pain and confliction.

I wanted to cry but could not bring myself to cry.

I felt all sorts of things inside me, however it all felt like a blur.

Then came the day of the funeral. The whole family was there. All my uncles, aunts, and cousins from both sides of the family had come to support us as we said our final goodbyes. I do not remember much of exactly what was said during the service, but I do remember the song that played as the coffin was lowered into the floor and the curtains were drawn. It was Brian Adam's, *"Everything I Do, I Do It For You."*

KISS OF TAOWAY

I stood there, numb. Listening to a song I loved, whilst I felt such pain I could hardly breathe. I saw Mum and Dad holding each other, my sister, and her husband together, my brother in the arms of his girlfriend. I looked and looked for someone to hold me, to tell me it is going to be ok. Then I looked at my aunty Maureen, she put her arms out and I fell into them.

Wow, the emotions hit me like a tidal wave; they erupted in sobs as I let out all that pain.

Even now, I feel the tears well up and the gratitude I have that she was there to help me at that time.

Lots of things changed after this. I gained my Early Childhood Education qualification, got married and had three, amazing children. I grew a lot in many aspects of my life. And for a long time, I was happy.

I really do think that there is no pain like the pain of losing a loved one.

The next significant event that would send me into the biggest spiral of my life, came the night my marriage ended. After we decided that it was time to separate, I drove home.

Before leaving our marriage counselling session, I messaged my Mum saying, *"Mum, I need you. Can you come over in 20 minutes? Text don't call."*

As I was driving home, I had to put all my efforts into concentrating on what I was doing. Every set of lights I stopped at, every single one, I burst into tears. I was absolutely devastated.

Somehow, I made it home. I went inside and the first thing I did was make myself a Chai Latte. By the time it was ready, there was a knock at the door. I opened the door, let Mum in, and burst into tears all over again, explaining to her what had just happened.

Mum was my rock. She immediately said that I had a room at their place if I needed it. We chatted for about an hour, before Mum went home, and I went to bed. Alone.

The next morning, I rang to let Mum know I was ok. I knew that suicide is a huge risk factor for men in this situation and I wanted to assure her I was fine. Mum was out and I spoke to Dad who gave me some sound financial advice and let me know he was there to support me. This is advice I would share with anyone facing the same situation.

If you find that your relationship has ended, and you have a shared bank account, you need to immediately open up a new personal account and put some money in it. I am not suggesting closing down the joint accounts immediately, but you do need to make that one big financial shift. It removes a major bargaining hurdle you could be faced with if everything goes sour.

Within a week, I had moved into Mum and Dad's house and within a few weeks, I had removed all my belongings. I made this decision in order to give my children as much normality in a totally abnormal situation. The only thing now was to work out how I was going to see my three children.

Over the next few months, I saw two of my children, one at a time on alternate weekends. We had some great times. My eldest child refused to see me once I stopped going to the family dinner.

KISS OF TAOWAY

Both my eldest daughter and my son have autism, which has made the marriage break up even harder for them to understand.

This continued for several months until I was eventually taking my twins out together once a fortnight. It was great to be able to relearn how to be a father.

However, the turmoil that my separation had created within me, was nothing compared to what was to come.

Around six or seven weeks after my separation, I arrived back at Mum and Dad's after work one day. My mum said she needed to speak to me. I put my things away and came back. Mum proceeded to tell me that dad had been feeling unwell and had recently gone for a scan. The scan showed that he had spots on his liver. He was having a follow up appointment a few days later to find out exactly how bad it was.

By the next week, Dad had been given a diagnosis of stage four liver cancer. When I heard this, I was gutted. Here was my *"Superman"* Dad, and we had just been told he was going to die. I just wanted to scream, and I think at some point, I did.

I immediately went for a walk and listened to my music, as I do when I am very stressed or upset. I attempted to call my sister; however, she was still at work and uncontactable.

I became very destructive in several ways.

I had been playing around with *Plenty of Fish* and other dating apps because I felt I needed someone to complete me. I realise now that my constant searching and getting snagged by people was a way of trying to cope with so much that seemed out of my control. I had also made some financial misjudgements, getting scammed a couple of hundred dollars, but caught on and stopped it before it got too bad.

In hindsight, I realise that I was again looking outside myself, rather than within, to find the fulfilment I desired.

However, looking back on this time, I can see a huge cherry on top of that bitter cake. It brought our family much closer together. My sister moved down from Goulburn and worked from home remotely. I was back at home, helping Mum and Dad where I could. I was going shooting with my brother occasionally, as well as fishing.

One weekend, I picked my son up and headed down to Point Leo to meet up with my brother, his kids and Dad. It was such a simple afternoon; however, I know it meant a lot for Dad and I carry that memory with me always. I hope my son still treasures that memory. The kids all played in the sand, digging holes, and burying each other, or throwing frisbees and balls around. Dad and my brother meanwhile were sitting chatting and watching the fishing lines. Not one of us actually caught a fish, but that, of course, was not the point.

About a month later, it was planned that the family would take a trip to Puffing Billy. This was a fantastic day as Dad had his wife, three kids and two of his five grandchildren with him. We were lucky to have an amazing hostess who boarded with us. After learning of Dad's illness, she made sure we had a car to ourselves, as well as got us some water from the staff supplies when we got to Lakeside. It was great to see Dad smile and spend time with his grandkids, reminiscing about working at Cardinia Reservoir when he worked for the Board of Works.

KISS OF TAOWAY

My only regret is that my children missed out on spending this very special time with their Grandad.

Dad spent time teaching me how to make a budget on Excel, so I could learn to manage my own financial affairs. I can say that almost two years later, I am finally getting it all under control.

I remember one day, sitting with Dad out the back, just listening to the birds. I so wanted to tell him that day that I was so proud of how he was handling all of this, his imminent mortality. However, we spent most the time in silence. It is a special place; and I feel him near me whenever I am there or whenever I am gardening.

Christmas Day was a big one, as we all came together. I am so grateful that Dad was able to see four of his grandchildren one last time, before he went to hospital.

Thinking back now, that time was all a blur of emotions.

On one hand, I was reeling from the end of my marriage, but I was also having to deal with the inevitable prospect of saying goodbye to my Dad. It was during this time, within a week or two of my separation, that I returned to the Spiritualist Churches that I had been part of over ten years before. It is in reconnecting with spirituality in the way that I have, that I was able to deal with the pain and emotions that were coming up during this time.

The next couple of weeks were the hardest of my life, but also the most treasured. I watched as the love between the members of my family grew to such a level, I have heard members of the extended family praise how close we are.

TAO OF CHANGE

That is wonderful to hear; I am blessed that we are all together.

I only stayed with him alone one night, whilst he was in hospital. That was a very testing time. It was all going well, until in the middle of the night he started calling to me, *"John. John."* I responded, and he said, *"Go and get them."*

I asked, *"Who?"*

Dad replied, *"Huey, Dewey and Louie."*

I had been doing some reading about the process of passing and disorientation was one of the things I had read about. I went and found the nurse and in tears and told them what was going on. The nurses helped to settle him down.

The time that stands out as most significant for me, in its power of change, occurred just after the family had taken Dad outside for a short walk to see his dog, Danny. My sister and I had returned with Dad to his room and were helping him. Suddenly, I became overwhelmed with emotion and instead of bursting into tears in front of Dad, I quickly left the room.

I remember walking over to the small divider wall and resting my elbow on it as I cried. Then I remember the poem, *"Footprints."*

At this point, I lifted my head and prayed to my God, to Spirit, *"If ever there was a time I needed you to carry me, now is the time. Please lift me up in your loving embrace."*

By the time I finished praying, I was overcome with a sense of peace and calm. At this exact same time, my sister came out to see if I was ok. I explained what happened and that I was fine.

KISS OF TAOWAY

The days seemed to pass from one to another, with Dad steadily getting worse. Many times, I would just sit there with my hands on him, giving him some spiritual healing. Or I would stand back whilst others were with him and send healing to them so that they could do what they had come to do.

I was beginning to learn that everything happens for a reason.

Sometimes we are not meant to know why.

Other times we need to work out why.

The reason is always something significant for the individual. As I am discovering, all we need to do is stop. Take a step back and look at things from a different or wider perspective.

There is always a lesson, if only we are willing to be open to receive it.

It is incredible to see where I am now, compared to where I was at the beginning of 2018. It was January 5th when Dad died, surrounded by his loving wife and three children.

Although losing Dad was gut wrenching, it had a silver lining. The silver lining was how it brought the rest of us back together and we are all going strong to this day. Dad told my sister that he did not have any regrets. That is one thing that has inspired me. I do so many things now that I would not have done either before my separation or before Dad died. I now look for opportunities to embrace life, try new things and am even learning to take "*calculated*" risks. Calculating was not always my strong point.

Upheavals in life are unavoidable.

TAO OF CHANGE

Eventually we all face events that are so significant they can change who we are. I like to think of them as if they are chipping away at the old me, making way for a better, more refined me. As a stone mason chips away at a piece of stone with a gavel and chisel to create a masterpiece, I believe these epochal events are doing the same with us. However, it is in our hands to decide whether we go with it or not.

When we fight against change, we miss the lesson.

When we miss the lesson, we remain stagnant. When we are stagnant, the lesson returns, time and time again until we have learnt it. From my experience, when we ignore these lessons, the Universe sends them back to us time and again, becoming more and more significant until we have learnt them. This is where tuning into your synchronicities can help.

Synchronicities are just lessons that you have listened to and responded. As a result, you can evolve. This brings us to when we embrace the change.

Change is inevitable.

As sure as night follows day, and that we all must pay taxes. Change is something we all must embrace. But change does not need to be a big thing. Start with changing how you do something small. Then make that change a little bigger. With a little practice, you can change anything you want, from a perspective to a career, to where you live.

One final point. Although you may be tuning into your synchronicities and following them, this does not mean that epochal type events will not happen in your life. In cases like this, I believe it is the Universe pushing you to become more than you currently are.

It may be that you are cancelling out negative Karma, or it may be that on a soul level, you have chosen to come and experience this event to further develop on that much deeper level. Whatever the reason is, embrace it.

Embrace the opportunity to take a good long look at yourself and ask yourself, *"Am I happy with who I am?"*

Chapter 5

TAO OF FREEDOM

Life changing events can bring the best and the worst out of us.

Sometimes this is where our best learnings come from. Whether it be understanding why you erupted like Mount Vesuvius during a disagreement or succumb to temptation hiding in a scam. Here you will learn how to steer clear of some of the traps I fell into, during the darkest period of my life, and how to avoid them yourself.

To give some context, I had just come out of a 14-year marriage and moved home with my parents, and my father was diagnosed with Stage Four Liver Cancer.

KISS OF TAOWAY

During this time, I was in a real dark place. I was in deep despair, not only reeling from the end of my marriage, but also at the prospect of losing my father. I was torn between working out how to be a good father, whilst at the same time, trying to figure out how I could support my parents during this most difficult time.

I began looking outside myself for comfort, rather than within. This seems to be the default for many people, until they begin to connect with their true self and align with the Universe. I signed up for a dating app within a couple of weeks, thinking that I would not be able to meet anyone else. In hindsight, I realise this was way too early. However, at the time I was attempting to heal a broken dream I had had, of growing old with the love of my life.

Looking back now, I can see that I was a desperately broken young man, unfortunately the perfect target for scammers.

I received a contact from who I thought was a lovely lady. We spent two weeks chatting via messages, after taking things offline very quickly. That should have been the first red flag. This lady told me she wanted to meet up but was going to South Africa for work.

We kept contact whilst she was away. However, one day she messaged me asking if I would send her money. The photo she sent of her in a hospital bed, supposedly after being mugged looked very suspicious. In the photo, she was smiling quite happily, which was contrary to the tone in her message.

Luckily, I realised that I was being taken for a ride. I learnt then, that if you must use a dating site to meet people, keep it on the site until you have met and are comfortable to continue to get to know each other and further commit to a relationship. If you go offline too early, it is easier for scammers to get to you.

I was very lucky this time. However, it was not just in relationships that I was looking for something to help me feel better.

I saw a post on *Facebook* which talked about how these guys made a heap of money on cryptocurrency and had turned down big money from one of the Sharks on *Shark Tank*. After some initial enquiries, I decided to invest some money into this system to make some extra money.

After an initial investment of $250.00 ($300.00 AU), I began playing the game. It was all going well. The first few days I made slight increases. A few days had minor losses but I was still ahead. After a few weeks, the advisor said I could increase how many things I was investing in and that was when it all came crashing down. Overnight, I lost the $500.00 AU or so that I had made. I stopped investing for a couple of weeks.

One day, I decided to attempt it again, with a little more money to make money like I was initially, but quicker. However, my bank blocked the transaction. I received a message from my bank, so I called them and found out that the institution I had been working with was not recognised in Australia.

After this, I did more enquiries and discovered that the whole thing was a scam, using *Shark Tank* as its launching pad. Since then, I have seen the same scam numerous times using people like Mel Gibson to endorse cryptocurrency.

All this time, there was a little voice who kept saying to me, *"You need to rediscover who you are. Focus on finding out what makes you happy."*

KISS OF TAOWAY

This was my sister. Or at least the words she had said to me on several occasions. We had become really close again through supporting each other through our Dad's passing and as I learnt to live life as a single, forty-something year-old man.

However, as with many people, I had to learn the hard way.

I had fallen prey to *Plenty of Fish* and to the *Facebook* scam. I had only begun to start looking within, however, I still felt that my salvation was outside of me.

Within days of my separations, I found a self-help group on Facebook called Single Mums and Dads Support; SMADs for short. This was a great place to share experiences and learn from other parents in a similar situation.

I chatted with a few Mums on there, and eventually began dating a lovely Mum of four kids.

Everything was fantastic at the start, as it always seems to be. Magical and entrancing. However, there was that little voice inside of me that had listened to my sister, who kept saying, *"Who are you and what do you want to do?"*

After a few months together, I was able to start looking for a new place to live. This lovely lady helped me to find a few places that I was interested in.

A few weeks later, I found my new home, had put an offer in after showing it to my twins and began the long journey to owning my *own* place. It felt like no time had passed when I finally moved in.

Shortly after moving in, I went to Goulburn to help my sister pack. We had many discussions about spirituality, what our goals were and what we want to do in the future.

When I returned home, I realised I wanted to be at home in my own home. However, I felt I needed to keep visiting my girlfriend. This went on for a while, until eventually I began spending more and more time at home on my own.

Around June that year, I took my twins with me to the Peninsula Animal Aid and brought home two Chihuahuas, Molly and Maggie. Molly is 14 now and is the mother of Maggie, who is 13. Having two dogs of my own, a new home and lots of time to think, I realised I needed more me time. Unfortunately, I never actually came out and said that to my girlfriend. She stopped coming to visit me and we drifted apart.

It took quite some time, but finally I was starting to focus just on me. On whom I was and what I wanted to do. I did my archery, gardened, visited Grandma at the nursing home and my Mum and sister at their place. I went to my development circle and to the Spiritualist Churches. I was starting to understand what I wanted to do.

Around this time, I enrolled in a new healing modality; Pellowah, which means radical shift in consciousness. After the two days of training, I was a certified Pellowah Healer.

Pellowah is a beautiful healing modality, sent from the Angelic Realms. This modality focuses on the energetic and spiritual bodies, realigning the 12 strands of DNA and all the meridians, and balances all the chakras. The energy feels much lighter than

Reiki energy and is rather cold, compared to Reiki which is a much warmer energy.

Two days later, I had my epiphany when I was walking home from work about what I wanted to do with the rest of my life.

It was after a long day at the Kindergarten, and I was walking home, having spent all day with 30 five-year olds. I had excitedly shared with my team about my training and how I was looking forward to incorporating it into some sort of healing practice in the future.

Whilst I was contemplating this, on my walk home, I realised that I wanted to help people to discover their true calling, their purpose in life. I realised that I had been preparing for this for such a long time.

For as long as I could remember, I had embraced my spirituality.

For quite some time I had let it go, while I focused on the material things that required my attention. Now, I realised that what I wanted most was to incorporate my spirituality into every aspect of my life and in doing so, help others to find deeper meaning to their lives.

What drew me to Pellowah, was that it is a hands-off healing modality. Once you begin a healing session, you do not touch the client at all, working in their aura and treating their energy bodies. It is only when you have completed the healing session and ready to ground the client, that you quietly tell them you are finished and gently place your hands on the persons shoulder to bring them back. You may then want to use Reiki or other energy modalities to help ground the person after their Pellowah session.

TAO OF FREEDOM

Pellowah greatly compliments the spiritual healing that I am a channel for, as I often am directed to work solely in a person's energy bodies, rather than direct physical contact. Somehow, I know when contact is required and when it is not required.

The epiphany I had walking home had opened a proverbial Pandora's box inside of me.

I began several weeks of researching possibilities including Chaplaincy, Health and Wellbeing Coaching, before finally settling on a Diploma of Holistic Counselling. After receiving some much-needed spiritual guidance at the Seaford Church mini-expo through a reading with a gentleman called Matu Apiata, I was set.

Within a few weeks, I was enrolled and flying through the course material. Within six months, I had completed all the requirements, submitted all the case studies, and received my Diploma.

Whilst I was studying and working, I ended up on stress leave from work due to a complaint and I had informed work how I was struggling a lot with my mental wellbeing due to still working through my separation, not seeing my kids and my Father's death.

When I was on stress leave, I went back to my Pellowah teacher for attunements and the following week, I caught up with the student I did the course with. We exchanged Pellowah healings, and she invited me to her Laughter Yoga session the following week.

As it would turn out, Laughter Yoga was exactly what the doctor ordered. I felt my mood improve over the following couple of weeks whilst I was on leave and during the school holidays. We became good friends, and I would join her for Laughter Yoga twice a week at various locations.

After swapping Pellowah treatments again, I decided to let this lovely lady know that I liked her a bit more than friends. Unfortunately, she was not in a space to reciprocate this. It was then I realised that I needed to direct my search for love within.

I began a period of around three or four weeks where I truly focused on self-love, self-acceptance and discovering who I was on a deeper level. During this time, I read a lot and contemplated deeply about the self. It was also at this time that I was deep in my Diploma of Holistic Counselling studies. I discovered that self-love and self-acceptance are essential to truly finding love. Particularly the kind of love that seems to transcend the physical and become a truly spiritual union.

Oh, how that would be. To be with someone who can melt you just with a look, whilst at the same time support you to become all you can be.

Remember I said that I had decided to focus within to develop a sense of self-love and acceptance? Well, love came looking for me.

I was home on stress leave and relaxing at home when I received a message from a lady.

As it turns out, we had met earlier in the year when she had been coming to drop her grandson off at the Kindergarten where I taught. Initially, I rejected her contact respectfully, however a little voice told me that I should talk with her.

What followed was a huge series of little synchronicities, such as her being aware of spiritualism and being a very spiritual person herself. We spent quite some time messaging and chatting with each, and eventually we agreed to meet for coffee.

As it is our shared story, I believe this is not the time to share it. However, I will tell you that we are very happy and very much in love.

What I learnt in this period of my life was a fortunate lesson. Luckily, I learnt it quickly, as each time I went through it, the intensity strengthened.

I learnt that, "*I am enough.*"

I do not need a partner to be happy.

Yes, it is nice to have someone to share the ups and downs of life. However, it does not make you whole. I also learnt that when you truly begin to love yourself and accept yourself for who you are, anything is possible.

Once you love and accept yourself, the love you can find with another is more intense than anything you can possibly imagine.

Chapter 6

Tao of Learning

Although I had to learn many things the hard way, I also decided that I was going to make sure that I tried all sorts of new things whilst I was on this journey of rediscovery.

I remember one day, shortly after my separation, that I decided that I would try new things. If an opportunity to experience something new came along, I would.

Initially, this was in the form of the types and varieties of foods that I ate. I have tried many new foods in the past two years; many more than I had exposed myself to in my entire lifetime before then.

Exploring food was an easy way for me to explore who I was, as ultimately, we all need to eat.

Other things I decided to do were enrolling in the Spiritualism Course with the Victorian Spiritualist Union to understand the philosophy, religion, and science that I had embraced for many years and had just recently come back to. I also decided to learn archery, the art of camping, firing a rifle and fishing with my brother.

It was not until I purchased my new home did I begin to again immerse myself in the art of Bonsai and to start refocusing on and caring for my plants that I had neglected for so long. Over time, I created an entirely new vegetable garden.

Exploring old and new interests helped me to get a better understanding of what I was interested in, as well as what I was passionate about. I discovered very quickly that spirituality was key to everything I was doing. Not following the path of a dogma plagued religion, created by man in the image of God.

Rather a spirituality of self. Learning how to quieten the mind to be able to focus on what I was doing, as well as to be able to receive inner guidance from my higher self and my spirit guides.

Some aspects of this new understanding I had within myself came quickly; other aspects took time to develop. I am still learning to this day.

To clarify this some more, let us start with exploring food.

Shortly after moving back in with Mum and Dad, I noticed a vast difference in the meals we were having. To start with, we were having a fresh cut of meat every day. Either chicken, pork, or beef. Sometimes fish, but that was more as a treat when we had fish and chips. Then with every meal we would either have some cooked vegetables, or a fresh salad.

I love salads. So much you can do with it, using so little. A little bit of lemon juice, balsamic and a drizzle of olive oil and you can make a beautiful dressing for a meal.

This got me thinking about how I wanted to shop for food when I finally got my own place. Many celebrity chefs will tell you to shop on the peripherals of the supermarket. Fresh produce, the meat and egg section, cheese, and dairy sections. Frozen veggies are great as well as they are snap frozen, so they keep most of their nutrients.

Generally, I avoid the internal aisles unless I am looking for olive oil, herbs and spices or bread and cereal. I cannot sit here and say I never splurge and buy highly processed foods like chips, lollies, and biscuits, but I can say I limit these to only if I feel like them. They are not an essential in my household and will not be anytime soon. Like everyone, I enjoy some of the nicer things in life. I prefer to buy a good coffee or herbal tea, or even some soda water instead of a soft drink.

Continuing with the food exploration, a good friend, his son, and wife took me out for lunch. He had helped me to get my home and had been a great support during my separation. He offered to buy lunch for me. One of the foods I had put on my to-eat list was Kangaroo. I had previously turned Kangaroo down, but on this particular day, I went for it. And I am so glad I did. It was so tasty, and I would recommend it to anyone. In fact, I have made pasta sauce with it with my partner, and it tasted even better than when I use beef.

KISS OF TAOWAY

Time went on and my partner and I went to her friend's house. Her friend spent an afternoon teaching us how to cook traditional Sri Lankan food. This was a great experience, in particular, eating a freeze-dried, fried white chilli. Mmmm, it makes my mouth water just thinking about it!

I had been familiar with using traditionally European herbs such as Mint, Rosemary, Thyme, Oregano and Sage. Learning to use traditional Sri Lankan spices and herbs was a new twist on an old skill. Now my partner and I relish in spending an afternoon making up a curry. I explained to my Counsellor, that it is almost like we are engaged in a dance when we cook together. We both have different roles to play and share the flavours to make sure that we have it just the way we want it.

We've also shared a few laughs along the way, such as when I cut up one of the black seed chillies my partner's friend gave us. I used rubber gloves like I had been told, as these chillies are very hot. I only cut up one chilli, and by the end, I noticed one of the fingers had a hole in it. I decided to try out the chilli and touched my finger to the juice on the chopping board. I reached up and touched the same finger to the tip of my tongue. It was fine at the start, however, gradually over the next fifteen minutes the heat grew and grew. I am so glad I did not take a big lick. That little touch on the tip of my tongue was just about bearable. My partner and I laughed very hard, as I waited for the heat to subside.

We have had some rather interesting combination of food, and I love it. Adding cut up apple, pear, kiwi or even watermelon to a salad. What an explosion of flavours!

On another occasion, we had two dishes made by my partner's friend, one was a fish dish, and the other was oxtail. The fish dish was very salty and went down well. The oxtail, on the other hand, took some mind power. I do not know why, but it took a bit for me to wrap my mind around eating a tail of an ox. It tastes nice - it is just the fact it was the tail.

I had a similar experience years before when I was served beef cheeks. This does not make sense as I can catch, gut, scale and clean fish and eat them whole or filleted. I also can eat the wings and drumsticks of chicken and turkey without any problem. So, what was the issue with the oxtail? I put it all down to being in my head.

I was able to put the fact that it was a tail out of my mind and focus on the flavour and texture, which was very pleasant. So much so, that when we went back several months later, I was able to eat the oxtail without any hesitation.

All new experiences can be daunting.

They are stressors in our lives. It is up to us to decide how much of an impact we allow that stress to cause. As a kindergarten teacher and a parent, I have seen firsthand many times the impact that food can have on children.

Research and evidence explain and cite the impact different additives can have on the human body.

Bill Statham's *"The Chemical Maze Shopping Companion"* book is a guide I used for a long time to help understand the impact of food on my psoriasis. It is ultimately a simple list of additives and their safety ratings and potential impacts on health.

So, why am I mentioning this?

KISS OF TAOWAY

Food is essential to our survival.

Without it, we will die. Our body is made up of cells which require nutrients and those nutrients come from the foods we eat. When contemplating living a more spiritual existence, food was one of the first things I began to consider the impact on my whole being.

If I truly want to honour myself, I need to honour the food I eat. Is the food fuel for my body or am I eating to cover up an emotional or psychological need that I have not met? When I began to eat more mindfully, my love of food grew. I love tasting the complex flavours individually, as well as when they are combined. The aroma, as I cook or as I acknowledge thanks for what I am about to eat, prepares me for what is to come.

I will pose this question to you: Are you present when you eat?

Eating mindfully is an amazing experience.

When I sit down to eat a meal, I always take a moment. I smell the food. Look at it. I then close my eyes and either verbally or in my mind give thanks to the Universe for the food I am about to eat. I regularly do this same practice with my water, giving thanks in my mind to clear any negative energy or memory from the water before I drink it.

Japanese doctor, Dr Masaru Emoto describes is his book *"The Hidden Message in Water"* that water has memory, which is echoed by a speech that Sadhguru, an Indian mystic, talked about an old Indian tradition of bringing water in at night and not drinking it until the morning. He describes how the water collects memories from those it passes, as well as through the pipe system. Whether or not you believe in the theory put forward by both these men is up to you. However, I do suggest that giving thanks and blessings to our food and water cannot hurt.

If we want to look at things from a different perspective, everything is energy.

If we look at a pea or a drop of water under a microscope, if you zoom in enough, you will see electrons flying around a nucleus. This is one of the few scientific certainties; everything is made up of energy.

Now picture this. Your meal arrives. You observe the aroma and the look of the food. You bend closer to get a good smell. Then you close your eyes and breath in. In your mind, you thank your God, or the Universe for the food you are about to eat. Then you open your eyes and wolf the meal down. It is gone in mere minutes.

You have honoured the food, but not yourself.

Consider an alternative. You open your eyes and mindfully pick up your knife and fork. You observe the meal, as a whole, as well as the individual components. Can you detect certain herbs or spices? What else can you smell? Maybe butter melting on a corn cob or a hot dinner roll. You decide on the first item you want to eat, cut it, pick it up on your fork and lift it to your mouth. Instead of putting it straight in, you observe this tiny morsel, smell it again, before finally putting it in your mouth. The explosion of flavours enwraps you, as you place your fork down on the table and close your eyes.

You are immersed in the flavours and textures of that one piece of your meal. You chew repeatedly, noticing the different textures of the food, the flavours as they roll across your tongue. After what seems like an eternity, you swallow and relish the feeling as it slides down the back of your throat and into your stomach.

You open your eyes mindfully, pick up your knife and fork and repeat for the remainder of the meal. In this scenario, you are not only honouring the food you are eating, but you are also honouring yourself. You are fully immersed in the meal and allowing the assimilation of the energy from the food into your body to be achieved more effectively.

Honouring yourself comes in many forms. As mentioned at the start of the chapter, I committed to myself to try new things. Some of these I chose to do, like learning archery and going camping. Others I was asked to do, in the form of helping Mum and Dad out during those last few months.

Archery was the first thing I decided to try. I fell in love the first time I went to Frankston Archery Club for a come and try session. It was everything I imagined and more. After completing their beginner's archery course, I bought my first target shooting bow and arrow set.

That feeling you get when you shoot your arrow at a target and get it close to where you were targeting. It is a really great feeling. Beyond the immediate gratification I received when I started shooting, I found that it was a great way to destress.

In life, there are many things we have control over, and there are many things we do not. This is something I learnt from archery.

TAO OF LEARNING

I can control exactly where I plant my feet. I can control how I hold the bow. How I nock the arrow. How I hold the string and draw it back and then release it.

I cannot control the wind. I cannot control the air pressure or moisture in the air. Up until I release the arrow, I am in control. At the point I release the arrow, I must surrender to the elements; you could say to God or the Universe. Although I am still a beginner in my eyes, archery taught me a lot about life in general.

Being in the moment when I am shooting is a significant feeling. I find it best to do it when I am the only person there, however, sometimes that is not an option. I can enter my shooting with a huge worry on my mind and within a few arrows, I am shifting my thoughts away from those worries and focussing on what I have control of.

I would love to say that I was able to solve all my problems with archery, but that would not be truthful. Also, I do not believe that there is any silver bullet that can solve all your problems. That is why I always ask myself, "*Why is this happening?*" and "*What am I learning from this?*"

I do not always get an answer, however, like with my archery, I am able to gather some new learning about myself if I just take the time.

The other thing I have become quite accomplished at, is minor constructions. Within a week or two of moving into to Mum and Dad's, they had bought a new bed for me. In the past, I had always been the *Gofer*. Go for this, go for that. Dad, on the other, had asked me to put the bed together as he was not able to. After a little trial and error, I put the bed together. With just a little guidance from Dad, here and there.

This led to more opportunities to learn new skills, such as when Dad got me to climb a ladder to spray the pear leaf to kill off the curly leaf caterpillars, or when Dad gave me the 101 on starting and maintaining the lawnmower.

Realising that I was capable of putting together pack furniture gave me a lot of confidence. Since then, I have helped my Mum, sister, partner, and colleagues at work put together items, ranging from glass display cabinets to kitchen tables, bunks, and greenhouse; I even set up my own target for archery during the Covid-19 pandemic lockdown.

Learning to do new things helps you to see a new version of you.

You can see what you might be able to do with a new skill and what possibilities for learning may open for you. After all, is that why we are here. To learn during our physical life.

Regardless of whether you believe in God, or an afterlife for that matter, imagine life if you were not able to learn. I do not know about you, but I am sure I would go crazy if I was not able to learn and experience new things in life.

Learning does not need to be formal education.

Read a book, a blog, or a newspaper. I am sure you can still get newspapers somewhere around here. Talk to friends, colleagues or even a stranger. Discuss a variety of different topics.

TAO OF LEARNING

Something I did to further my learning was join *Toastmasters*. My sister had introduced me to this wonderful organisation, and I have been loving it ever since. It is an amazing way to learn something new, whilst at the same time socialising with amazing people who want to help and support you.

Exploring new opportunities in life, whether that be food, people, places, or experiences, is essential to help you to understand who you are and what you are going to do with your life.

Investing in yourself is the key to knowing who you are.

Chapter 7

TAO OF SELF

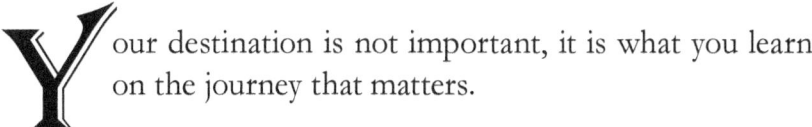

Your destination is not important, it is what you learn on the journey that matters.

Ultimately, if we were to move directly from Point A to B and expect things to change, nothing would change; that is unless we take heed of what happens on that journey.

I think this entire spiritual journey has been one of the most riveting times of my life.

Through a great deal of hardship, self-reflection, and contemplation I have been able to really learn a lot about myself. By facing the challenges of life and looking within, I have gained a greater understanding of who I am and what I want to achieve in life.

KISS OF TAOWAY

As a Kindergarten Teacher, I have often told parents when discussing their children's development and learning, that it is the process they go through when learning new skills, more so than the finished product.

For a child, sticking one piece of cotton wool onto a piece of paper could be a huge achievement. Firstly, they have had to organise the materials they required, then they have to find a place to work. They have to choose how to hold the glue brush and the cotton wool, how to put the glue on and press the cotton wool onto their chosen medium.

As an adult, we often forget about the complexities of learning that children go through; that we too have gone through.

It is through self-reflection that we can take a step back and look deeper at ourselves to understand why and how we are doing the things we are doing. We can also use this process to understand how and why we have developed certain behaviours, as well as commencing work to modify our behaviour so that it is more aligned with our higher self, values, and beliefs.

My period of rediscovery came after the breakup of my 14-year marriage and the death of my Father. I was not a happy person. I had been struggling with Generalised Anxiety Disorder for at least six or seven years. My nerves were always on edge, I struggled in my relationship with my children and my wife.

When my marriage ended, I looked immediately at myself. What had I done? What could I have done differently? I will not go into details why I think our marriage ended, besides to say that "communication is key".

TAO OF SELF

I lost my voice, figuratively. I could not talk about how I felt or why I was struggling. In many ways, it was because I did not know the answer to either of those questions at the time.

As we know, all relationships are based on good communication. Whether it is a romantic, friendship or work relationship, communication is the key to a positive relationship. Ensuring that all parties can communicate their ideas, feelings, and beliefs safely and without judgement is essential to building good relationships.

This is where I started my rediscovery. I began to look at my values and beliefs and what I felt was essential for a happy life. For my happy life.

I spent numerous hours talking to my Mum and Dad, my sister, my Counsellor, colleagues, and a few friends about what I valued and what my beliefs were. I cemented these into my mind. It dawned on me, that all my core beliefs were focused on spirituality. Living in accordance with my spiritual beliefs, incorporating spirituality into my day-to-day life and working in accordance with my spiritual beliefs. Further to this, I realised that connection with family, having fun, living a sustainable, healthy, and mindful existence.

Yes, my spiritual beliefs are very different from many, but that is because most of the people I grew up with were of a Christian faith. That was until I joined my Grandma at Mornington Church one Sunday and everything changed.

I discovered the world of Spiritualism and thought, *"Wow, these people have similar beliefs to me."*

KISS OF TAOWAY

It was a real game changer.

One aspect of Spiritualism is that they have no set doctrine, so you can come from any faith and still follow Spiritualism. The other aspect is that each Spiritualist is only expected to believe in verifiable fact and personal experience. As such, you are encouraged to explore your own spiritual journey along the path with those you are travelling. Sometimes we diverge and take different paths, but that is because we require a certain experience to help us understand.

However, the path leads to our final awakening upon our mortal death.

This is where a great deal of my self-discovery and understanding of who I was came from. When I began to look at the events of my life and started asking myself, *"What am I meant to learn from this?"* or *"What is this teaching me?"*, I began to really start to see changes in how I was reacting at the moment and began to move towards being more responsive. I realised that reacting was very instinctive and done very much out of self-preservation; whilst responsiveness means you take time to consider what is happening and think and plan an appropriate and applicable response.

Looking deep within myself, I had my belief in the continuation of the soul after the physical death reaffirmed several times. This was a comfort for me. As a result, I was able to come to peace that certain people I cannot see at the moment, because I know that when we all pass beyond the veil, I will be able to hold them again in my embrace and tell them that I never stopped loving them.

TAO OF SELF

This is not to say that it makes missing my Father or other people who have died or moved out of my life any easier. However, it does make it easier to cope with, due to my strong belief of life after death, and that one day we will be together again.

The other thing I learnt when I reconnected with my spiritual self and path, was that I wanted to work with people and help them to discover who they are and what they want to do with their life.

Through my studies, I have learnt skills that will enable me to work with individuals and groups of people in a counselling role, as well as coaching, mentoring, guiding people to find their own answers to their own predicaments.

I am not entirely sure where this is taking me, however, I am loving the journey.

Having taken care of myself through honouring myself with the food I ate, I began the deeper journey of focusing on my thoughts, beliefs, and values. This was one of the first steps I took in beginning to honour and love myself.

By focusing on these attributes specifically, I was able see what my internal narrative was saying to me and how I was eventually able to shift many of those beliefs and replace them with positive views of myself or specific situations.

In many respects, I was doing what we are told not to do as children, as well as adults. That is learning to put myself first.

During my career as a Kindergarten Teacher, I have been working thirty-eight to forty hours a week. In the first 10 years, I had been travelling up to forty-five minutes to and from Southland to work in a Child Care Centre with thirty, three to five-year-old children. It was an exhausting period where I got married, had children, and did my best to develop both as a professional and as a Father. This left little time for me to concentrate on my relationship with my wife - or myself.

When I managed to successfully land a position with the local council as a Kindergarten Teacher, I thought the shorter commute would make the difference. However, it did not. I fell back into many of the old habits and behaviours that I had used to cover my anxiety.

Almost ten years down the track and I was finally ready to face my inner dialogue and have some very deep discussions.

This started with a counselling session I had with Bronwyn. However, this just began the snowball effect of self-reflection.

One of the biggest obstacles I had to face was my negative self-image and self-defeating beliefs. I had been convinced by my past that I was not a good Father, that I was perceived as being an angry Dad, that I was not a good teacher, I had let my family down, and many, many more beliefs that I had to overcome. Many beliefs I had taken on either from other people and what they said, or by following untrue narratives I told myself to justify why I felt the way I did.

As soon as my marriage ended, and I had grieved enough that I could start making good choices, I enrolled in a *"Parenting After Separation"* course with *Relationships Australia*. I discovered that I was not the only person who had had these tough experiences and self-image problems and that I would be able to work through them.

TAO OF SELF

Whenever I speak to people about my experiences or about their experiences, I always say that there is never cause for violence.

Violence comes from a place of disharmony.

When we are tired, hungry, sick, exhausted, anxious, or scared we are more likely to respond in more aggressive or even violent ways than if we are rested, well fed, healthy and in a calm and peaceful place.

This is something I began to learn about myself.

I understood that if I was not aware of how I was feeling, then the tendency to be reactive was much higher. However, with lots of practice in mindfulness, meditation and checking in with myself, I can be more responsive in challenging times during my life.

I have also learnt, through a lot of trial and error, that I cannot let myself be influenced by the behaviours of others. That I have no control, nor power over what they do and how they do the things they do. There is only one person I have control of, and that is myself.

Only I can control my thoughts, beliefs, and feelings. To do this, I must first release the illusion of control outside of myself.

Releasing the illusion that we have of control over the world around us is very challenging. At the time of writing this, the world is under lockdown due to the Covid-19 pandemic. There are many things that are happening in the world today that are causing a lot of concern and inner turmoil. People refusing to wear masks, members of our society not isolating when they are infected and risking the health and wellbeing of everyone around them, and the general unease of not knowing what is going to happen next – or where the journey is going.

On the one hand, I am choosing to listen to what is going on, so I understand the restrictions and rules. On the other hand, I am consciously making sure that I do not take the fear and concern deep inside me and internalise it. My partner and I spend a lot of time discussing what is going on, our concerns, and helping each other to come up with solutions to how we are feeling.

You may be feeling overwhelmed with this feeling of having lost control. Several people have been making claims they have had their human rights removed. There is not much we can do at the present, besides look after ourselves and those we live with.

This brings us back to what you do have control over. You have control over what you watch and listen to, what you think, what you eat, whether you exercise or not, and how you feel.

Whenever you are faced with a traumatic experience, you must first take care of yourself.

First put on your oxygen mask, before you put on anyone else's. Make the change inside first. Only then will you be in any position to help make a change around you.

I know that if it rains, I cannot stop it by willing it. I know that there is famine, war, and disease in the world, and I cannot stop this by will alone or by worrying about it. To be able to change any of this, I must first make a change within myself.

TAO OF SELF

By creating a positive internal environment that is conducive to growth and evolving inwardly, only then can I make a change that may influence the outside world.

What I learnt very quickly was that when I was feeling positive, happy, and calm, I was also attracting those types of situations around me in the world as I went about my life. I had beautiful experiences learning Pellowah and made friends with the facilitator and student I did the course with. I discovered Laughter Yoga, Toastmasters, and my joy for Archery. I even met my partner, when I had reached a point where I decided that I would focus on self-love.

It was only when I had reached a point where I realised I did not need anyone in my life to fulfil me, that I met the love of my life.

So far, I have discussed how I have honoured myself through the food I prepare and eat, the deep learnings from the *"Men's Behaviour Change"* program and how I learnt to let go of worries I have no control of and focus on my own inner dialogue and creating positive change.

Practice what you preach; this is a saying I remember from my childhood. I embraced this wholeheartedly when I moved into my new home. I set up my own refuse station with a variety of bins for different types of rubbish. What I have found is that it is quite easy to set up a sustainable environment if you just put the time and effort in.

Firstly, I dedicated a bin to soft plastics, which, when it is full, I take it to *Woollies* to be sent to *Red Cycle* to get turned into play equipment and outdoor furniture. Then I have a recycling bin. This is the largest of the bins, as majority of our rubbish goes into this bin. Finally, I have a rubbish bin. Sometimes, this is not even filled in a week.

I received a compost bin from my Mum who had a spare one and have this running continuously. The compost, when it is ready, is put onto one of my six vegetable patches where I grow a variety of vegetables, including tomato, radish, silverbeet, broccoli, carrots, zucchini and cucumber. This is in addition to a large variety of herbs such as sage, thyme, oregano, mint, basil, and my favourite, rosemary. The only thing I am missing is a worm farm, however, this is something I plan to purchase very soon.

One realisation that I believe many of us have trouble with acknowledging is:

"You are enough."

They are the most powerful words I have heard. I've heard them from my sister on many occasions, during both individual coaching and in her *"It is my Life"* coaching circle. When she says this to me, she is often demonstrating that I am enough, that the person I have grown into over the past two years is vastly different than the person I was before. She is also pointing out that things that have been projected on me by others, are just a reflection of themselves.

When you look at yourself, do you cringe? Or, do you say, *"Hey there, how you doing? I am GREAT."*

This simple variation can have a huge impact upon how you perceive the world and managing the challenges that you face daily.

Chapter 8

Tao of Self-Honouring

ll I have learnt so far comes together under the age-old concept of *"Honour Thy Self."*

"Honour Thy Self" sums up the importance of knowing who you are at your core and living a life in harmony with your values.

Too often, people define themselves according to how others perceive them.

Whether that be family, friends, colleagues, the media, or even society. Not all of us will have the dilemma of facing every level of judgement, however the influence is still present.

Take for example the following scenario. You have a newborn child. What is the first question everyone asks you? Is it a boy or a girl? Have you ever really thought about the impact the answer you give people has on their interpretation of who your newborn baby is?

Through the child development studies that I undertook in my Early Childhood qualification, as well as through personal experience both as a parent and a professional teacher, the response generally goes something along the lines of the following, *"It's a boy."*

Here, people will often reply with things like, *"He's a strapping lad,"* or *"He has a strong set of lungs,"* or *"He'll be a heartbreaker!"*

Alternatively, if you say, *"It's a girl,"* the response is often along the lines of, *"Isn't she cute?"* or *"She is so beautiful,"* or *"Hello there, Princess."*

I am not saying that everyone will respond this way, however there is a strong tendency in our society to build boys up and objectify girls. There is no wonder we grow up being confused about who we are, when we have pre-set stereotypes imprinted upon us, because of our gender at birth.

Then adults we meet, begin to imprint upon us the behaviours and attributes we should strive for, according to our gender. Girls should play with dolls and boys should play with cars.

This is then backed up by media and marketing. I must admit that in the past few years, I have seen a slight improvement in the stereotyping that occurs in the media when it is focusing on children. We have seen an increase in programs which depict girls or women less as fragile victims and more as brave, compassionate and daring to defy the norm. We are seeing girls receiving role models in their programs that depict the female heroes and even superheroes. We are even seeing more female characters in roles traditionally held by men, such as mechanics, builders, and farmers.

Unfortunately, I cannot say I see this in the marketing industry. When you enter the toy sections of your favourite variety store, what colours do you see? I would like to be proven wrong, however whenever I go a to a toy shop, the boy's section is usually blue, and the girl's section is usually pink.

These have become synonymously identified as male and female colours, respectively. I am not sure about you; however, I am certain I have never visited a newborn baby who looks blue or pink. Neither have I ever known a blue before that is genetically male, nor a pink that is female. This is a concept that I challenge all the time as a Kindergarten Teacher. As I dress in rather colourful Hawaiian style shirts of every colour imaginable, I regularly get challenged by the children that say, *"You're wearing a girl colour"* when I am wearing a pink or purple shirt. In these circumstances, I often use it as a teachable moment, explaining to the children involved that colours are gender-neutral.

Ok, I will be as blunt as I can be, blue and pink are not born. They do not have genitals, something which legally determines one's gender at the present.

As a society, we have fought hard for gender equality (which is still ongoing), same sex marriage, indigenous rights, and freedom of choice. It is about time we start making a shift and start focusing on individuals as an individual, not as an individual assigned to a specific role due to the gender they are born.

KISS OF TAOWAY

An old theory on child development was that of a blank canvas as described by Psychologist B. F. Skinner who believed that children were born as a blank canvas and learnt through personal experience and conditioning. I am not saying that I agree or disagree with this, however, I would challenge you, next time you see a baby, to see them as an individual, upon which all of your preconceived notions will be etched. Then you may rethink the way you proceed to interact with the child.

In a perfect world, it would be possible for us all to grow up and learn who we are without the conditioning of society telling us who we should be. This is where *"Honour Thy Self"* comes in. Most people spend their lives on the endless spinning wheel of life, so to speak, fulfilling a role they do not like or understand.

Too often, we do not even recognise that we are fulfilling a specific stereotype, until a certain event causes havoc in your life and you are forced to look at what was right in front of you the whole time.

Often, as we approach a pivotal moment in our life, we can feel things changing, yet we do not know what they are. Sometimes these pivotal moments are blessings, such as the birth of a child or a marriage. These situations are usually filled with lots of planning, and this can often create the positive change you are looking for in your life, such as planning to quit smoking when you find out you're going to be a parent and taking all steps necessary to achieve this. You may decide to review your financial situation during planning for a wedding so that you can buy your first home or have that honeymoon you always wanted.

Then there are those pivotal moments that sneak up on you, such as a death, a relationship breaking down or losing your job.

In these situations, when you look back and reflect, they will often be proceeded by certain tell-tale signs that something is up. These may be periods of illness before a major health issue, more tension and arguments before a relationship break down, or more dissatisfaction at work.

When we are going through these phases, before the pivotal moment forces you to take account of who you are, we are often unaware that anything is happening and that it is all part of life as we know it. In some ways, I think it is all part of life as you know it. This is because it is how you have learnt to live after however many years you have been alive.

The challenge is to not let the pivotal moment prevent you from learning who you really are.

"Honour Thy Self" is a term my partner has used many times since we met in late 2019. My understanding of it is that we have only one life and we need to make the most of our life.

Life is meant to be a journey of joy and discover, and the best way we can achieve a truly happy life is to honour thy self.

During my experience of discovery and honouring myself, I began with a simple question. I put to myself, *"Who am I and what do I like to do?"*

I do not even think that I knew that I was honouring myself at the time. However, as time went on, I realised that this is exactly what I have been doing.

I have a greater understanding of who I am now, almost three years since that pivotal night. However, what I am here to achieve is constantly evolving and I do not know whether we ever have set things to achieve or whether the process of evolving through challenge, change and experience, is the whole purpose.

If it is the process of evolving with change, then I would think I am well on the way, yet very far from achieving it.

If our purpose is to experience life, then that is what I have been doing as much as I can ever since I began to question who I was.

Continuing with honouring myself, I decided that I wanted to create a purpose-built fire pit area to sit around a fire in the evening. This is a place I often feel I can think deeply and even use ceremoniously in remembering loved ones like my Dad, as well as giving prayers for healing others and for forgiveness.

The fire pit I have now is a far different one to what it started out as. Originally, I placed some large pavers on the grass, put some large logs around it and voila. Over time, I have added a frame and large pebbles to decorate the area and make it even more special for me.

I regularly make a fire at the end of the day, to sit around, sing and even reminisce. Sometimes I use the process of chopping wood as a stress reliever and then sit down listening to my favourite music and singing my heart out until the fire goes down.

Often, I will gather rosemary, tea tree, sage and other herbs and put them on the fire while I say a prayer. This is quite a comforting thing to do. I have done this for a long time.

The first time I think was when my Grandad died. My children did not come to the funeral as they were too young, so I dug a hole out the back and made a small fire. The children all wrote or drew a special message for him. Before we put these messages in the fire, I placed some gum leaves and rosemary in the fire. This was a very comforting moment with my children.

I often use fire in this way, as I have learnt over the years that many cultures use fire as part of their prayer rituals. From lighting a candle in a church, to using fire to heat up stones for a sweat lodge, fire has been a tool used to carry messages to places we cannot go.

Behind everything I have done to *"Honour Thy Self"*, the strongest notion is my spiritual connection. It is this notion of discovering who I am at the core of my being.

Beyond the flesh and bones, who am I?

I recently gave my first speech in a *Toastmaster's* competition. I had to answer the question, *"Who am I really?"*

One of the points I made is that I am energy. I know I am a physical being; I know I am a Father, a teacher, a partner. However, when I contemplate this all, and think about what makes me up, I see that I am made up of trillions of cells, each with a nucleus surrounded by electrons. Somehow, they have formed together to create the physical form that is John Ledgar.

Honouring yourself, does not mean you are being selfish. On the contrary, honouring thy self means you are investing in yourself so that you can be a better person. If you are a better person, for honouring yourself, this means you can give a better version of yourself to yourself and those around you.

KISS OF TAOWAY

Next time you see a newborn child, remember that. Remember to honour them for the person they are, not the person you think they ought to be. Although we cannot control what the wider community does, we can control how we hold ourselves and what we project on others.

Chapter 9

Tao of the Path

Having spent my whole working life as an employee in various fields, from refurbishing Myer Frankston to manual labour doing lawns, tying down windows onto truck scaffolds, to teacher aid work and finally, working as a Kindergarten Teacher; 2019 was the year I began to look at a new career path.

Having already been deeply focused on discovering who I am, undertaking Level 1 and 2 Pellowah Healing training and finally focusing on studying a Diploma of Holistic Counselling, I came one step closer to becoming my own boss.

My own boss. Being in charge of my own business. Wow, it sounds amazing right? It is but has also been fraught with challenges.

The first challenge was what I was going to do? Next it was who is my ideal client? And how was I going to bring it all to fruition?

This is the continuation of my journey of awakening and growing as a human, which encompasses what my business is going to be about. Being a guide for others who have been faced with traumatic events that have forced them to re-evaluate their own lives and work out who they are and what they want out of the remainder of their life.

Have I completed the first challenge? Yes, and no. Yes, I know the sort of work I want to do however, I am still processing how this will be undertaken.

As this is my story, all that I can offer anyone is what has worked for me. In this sense, those who are aligned with my journey and in a place to receive my learnings as a guide, will be guided to me through the synchronicity of life.

A large portion of what I do when helping people work through this challenge in their own life, is challenging thought processes and beliefs.

Coming back to values, I encourage clients to re-evaluate what and where their values lie.

Looking into your own values can give you a clear indication of where you are and where you want to be. Having a value does not necessarily mean we are living that value, however it can be a guide to help us to learn and understand how to live more in alignment with our values.

I had allowed the enjoyment of life to be lost, whilst I focused too much of my attention on the things that worried or stressed me.

How much time had I wasted through worrying about things happening? The other question I ask myself is related to the law of attraction and that is:

"How much of the life changing events did I influence or attract to me, merely by focusing my attention on the what if?"

I do not know if I attracted my separation, however I can see how some of my worrying behaviour did add to the final events that lead to the breakup. I do know that a lot of my worrying during my career has led to a point where I felt I had no choice but to consider changing careers.

Working with clients and challenging their limiting beliefs is also an aspect I relish in. I have seen the impact of challenging negative thoughts and reframing them in a positive way. One example of a negative belief I had developed, which my Mum helped me to reframe, was that *"I am a bad Father."*

This is a belief I had developed over many years. However, it only took a single conversation to reframe it. Whilst talking with my Mum, I was discussing how I was focusing on myself and who I am so that when I start to see my children again, they will see a *"New Dad."*

Mum said to me, *"You are making yourself a new and improved version of who you are."*

That simple concept helps so much during a time that is extremely difficult and trying.

Something I have often struggled with throughout my whole career, possibly even my whole life is the question: *"Am I good enough?"*

I am sure many of you have asked yourself this same question. Again, words of wisdom came to me from family again. It was during my sister's *"It is my life"* coaching session one night, that I was sharing my experience and self-doubt came in. I do not remember what I had been saying, however I remember the words of my sister Kaylene so clearly.

She said, *"John, you are enough."* Then she went onto giving examples of how I can help people with my meditation circle I conduct. She also mentioned things like my insight, compassion, and other strengths she saw. This was echoed by the other participants in the group.

Having a fear, we are not good enough, strong enough, attractive enough, or skilled enough is not a problem. Allowing that fear to dominate our life, is a problem. This is where personal experience comes into its own. What I mean here, is we are all experts at something. We are experts at being who we are.

Something I have mentioned to many people, on many occasions, is about the perspectives around cleaning at work. I raise this, because we all have our own perspectives on cleaning, our abilities, our roles and so on. The issue I point out here is that everyone will have a different perspective of how something should be done.

For example, let us consider cleaning paint jars at the end of a Kindergarten session. Some staff, myself included, are quite happy to top it up if required and then wipe the rim and put the lid back on. Job done. Now we can focus on other more important duties; more important to us, that is.

Other staff will insist on ensuring the paint pot is pristine and filled with new paint at the end of the day, taking extra time to clean the pot, and then clean the sink of the excess paint.

I am not saying that either way is better. I am just stating that everyone has a different perspective of how things should be done.

I usually go on to say that if an individual does not feel a role has been done to their specifications, then maybe it is their responsibility to complete that role to their standard. This all implies that we are all working towards a professional standard in the first place.

In life, everyone has their ideal insight into how things should be done. Whether that is in the work place, at home or in social settings. The point I am making here, is that we need to work to what we perceive to be the ideal level of whatever we are doing, rather than trying to complete that to a standard we believe others are holding.

Only through living to your own standard of life can you truly express yourself.

How I am approaching *"the fear"* is by tackling it front on. I guess that is how I face many of my own fears.

For example, when I was five years old, we were at Darling and Papa's house. We were out at the pool and I was afraid of the deep end. I loved playing in the pool but was not an accomplished swimmer. I usually hung to the edge of the pool.

KISS OF TAOWAY

This day, I decided I would tackle the deep end. I stood at the side of the deep end and called to Mum and Dad and my Grandparents, *"Look at me, I am Tarzan!"*

Then I jumped in the pool. I went down. Straight down to the bottom of the pool. Later, I learned that Mum said to my Dad, *"Dave, I don't think he's coming up!"* To which my Dad jumped in, fully clothed, and pulled me up by the hair on top of my head.

My hero.

I am approaching my fear of *what if*, with my business in the same way. Last year, I decided it was time that I began to teach others meditation. I focus on visualisation with my meditation and have several regulars who have been coming ever since. The greatest challenge was going virtual, when the Covid-19 pandemic put us all into lockdown.

Going virtual was a real challenge as it has been very difficult to find music or sound that you can play that does not get distracting through the online platforms such as *Zoom, Skype,* and *Webex*.

Another challenge is how can I make what I have experienced, into a practical usable format which will benefit others. This is a process I am currently still working on; this book being one of the tools that my clients will have access to.

The other challenge that I have faced are the trolls and haters through social media. Determining who is genuine and who is looking for someone to take the brunt of their frustrations is a challenge.

However, it is also a great learning opportunity. Learning not only how to pick those who genuinely need your assistance, whilst ignoring or diplomatically communicating with the non-genuine. Also, it teaches you a lot about yourself and how you can respond to these situations in a positive and caring manner, even when faced with adversity and hate speech.

The utmost importance to the learning I have been doing, both independently and with my sister, is the amount of time and effort it takes to set up a business. I am grateful that I set a five-year plan to transition from kindergarten teacher to a business owner.

Is it going to take me five years? Will it happen soon, or will it take longer than expected?

I do not have these answers. All I do know is it will happen in its own time and when it is ready. Even now, I know that I am on the right path.

Where that leads I do not know. Is my perceived destination where I am going to end up?

I do not know that, either. However, I do know that eventually I will be able to help many others, by sharing my own journey. I have something unique to me to share. A perspective or a flavour that only I can share. And when the time is right, share it I will.

The only other thing I know, is that I endeavour to keep things simple.

The KISS principle is something my Dad always referred to, and when I began considering creating a business to help people move on from adversity, it has been a concept I want to incorporate into my business.

For me, KISS means: Keep It Simple Solution.

And that is why this book is the KISS of Taoway.

We are all faced with all manner of experiences in life. This can often bring out a fair share of challenges. The premise of my Keep It Simple Solution, is that for every problem, there is always a solution.

Keep It Simple Solution points out that in most cases, the solution to our current situation is usual a simple solution. In most cases, it could be a simple decision, a change of perspective, or a simple action that can help us to resolve our challenges.

By beginning to look for simple solutions to our predicaments, we train ourselves to look for the simple, small things in life that can often lead us to a greater understanding and appreciation of life.

Even when we are faced with big challenges, we can still find those simple solutions to make our lives a little easier.

Getting up early to go for a walk, drinking more water, making the bed, or brushing your teeth regularly, could all be a simple solution to a current challenge you are facing.

When your obstacle or challenge is great, you may need many simple solutions. Regardless of whether your challenge is great or small, you can still find those simple solutions that will make each day brighter and more positive.

TAO OF THE PATH

Taoway is a name I created for myself several years ago. Tao, coming from the philosophy or religion of Taoism, translated roughly to *"The Way."* And Way, meaning *"Way,"* or a direction, path, or style of doing something.

I first learnt of Taoism through reading *"The I Ching"* in my late teens or early 20's.

The I Ching is based on the writings of Lao Tsu who wrote *"Tao Te Ching."* Taoism is attributed to the teachings of Lao Tsu. My first understandings of Taosim was a rough interpretation that a history teacher said during a History lesson whilst I was studying my Bachelor of Arts at Monash Clayton. He said that Tao roughly translated to, *"The Way"*.

Ever since then, I have been fascinated with Taoism and *"The Way"* as complimentary to my philosophical beliefs I have developed during my time as a follower of Spiritualism.

Hence, the name came to me one day during meditation; and the decision to call my book, *"The KISS of Taoway."*

Ultimately, the KISS of Taoway is about simple solutions that I have come up with to help get life back on track and to find more purpose and enjoyment in life.

I hope that within these pages, you are able to find little gems that will help you design the life you really want.

Chapter 10

Tao of Flow

At the beginning of 2020, writing a book was a dream I planned to fulfil in around two years' time. I had attended a couple of workshops where we were taken through creating vision boards. A vision board is like a visual goal or desire setting tool where you creatively use a variety of artistic tools such as drawing, collage, and writing, to depict your desires and goals for the future.

Little did I know early in 2020, that I would embark on the journey of a lifetime. Writing my first book.

What to write about? It was the biggest question I kept asking myself.

Before I began down the book writing path, I already had some ideas about what I wanted to do, moving forward in my life.

KISS OF TAOWAY

I have previously discussed how I learnt the Pellowah healing method, and this was to lead me to my first outing into my new life.

I was contacted late in 2019 by the President of the La Trobe Valley Spiritualist Church. Suzanne had read about my experience with Pellowah and invited me to do a workshop.

After a lot of planning and preparing an itinerary, I finally made it down to Morwell. My partner and my two Chihuahuas, Maggie and Molly, accompanied me.

We had prepared some art therapy activities, as well as an explanation and demonstration of Pellowah. That is where Maggie and Molly came in.

As I prepared to do the demonstration on Maggie in silence, everyone was very curious, observing my movements, but also how Maggie interacted with the energy.

Then it was time for Molly to have her turn, which I played the music that we are able to play when performing Pellowah. Maggie was with my partner but was eager to return to where I was demonstrating. She came over and sat still in front of me, fixated on the energy that was being shared.

In discussion after the demonstration, Suzanne asked if I could do a demonstration on one of the participants. This had not been agreed upon, as I did not believe I could do a demonstration given the strict guidelines we are taught during the Pellowah course.

I'm a stickler for the rules.

Finally, I agreed, after Suzanne said, *"I don't believe Spirit puts time frames on healing."*

With this in mind, and out of curiosity, I agreed.

The participant sat in the chair and I went to work in silence. I performed Pellowah in silence for about fifteen minutes. When we finished, she explained feelings of being cold all over and seeing rainbow colours. Other participants watching also said they could feel the coldness in the room, as well as seeing the energy flowing into the volunteer.

This was surprising to me, as it went against all I had learnt during my training, whilst at the same time confirming beliefs that I had had in the past, which Suzanne's comments stirred up inside me. Such as no one living knows what the spirit world is like. Many have beliefs or opinions, however there is no way to verify. Nor do I think we need it verified. That would take a lot of the faith out of spirituality.

As I write this, I am mourning the passing of my Grandma. However, I am also celebrating her life. She has been a great influence upon my spiritual journey. Grandma always reminded me that it is the Universe doing the work, we are the channels the spirits work through.

The rest of this workshop was focused around drawing therapy and creating prayer or meditation sticks. The participants all had a great time.

Then the Covid-19 pandemic hit. All of a sudden, my world, as well as everyone else's was turned upside down. I found myself, the same as everyone I knew, in uncharted territory.

KISS OF TAOWAY

I knew immediately that things were never going to be the same.

When I look back upon the last six or seven months, I am absolutely grateful for the experiences of the last few years. Not to mention the preparation I have been doing my whole life. Having spent the last two years, totally dedicated to improving and preserving my mental health and wellbeing, whilst at the same time developing my connection to Spirit, I had giving myself the best preparation for navigating an unexpected pandemic.

There is a common thought I have had for the duration of the pandemic, which is echoed by many people I have met on my spiritual journey. Covid-19 is the Universe's way of making us all stop and re-evaluate our lives and what is important to us.

I realised early on in 2020, that *today* is the most important day in my life.

Not yesterday, not tomorrow, but today.

Today is unlike any other day.

Today I am in charge of what I do, think, and feel.

I cannot change yesterday, and I am not able to influence tomorrow, until it becomes today.

During this time, I have learnt a lot about remaining in the present. By reminding myself to remain in the present, I learnt how to remain calm and focus on the things I had some degree of control over.

TAO OF FLOW

I remember reading an article on *Facebook* which was saying scientists had determined that the present is a measurable three-second window of time. Although there are some arguments about exactly how long the present is, I found this concept to be extremely comfortable and easy to incorporate into my own beliefs and philosophy on life and remaining in the present.

When situations of stress arrive, I can simply remind myself of the *"present three"* and focus on what I have control over. Often this is accompanied by returning my attention to my breath and if not that, to an activity I am presently doing such as chopping wood, digging, painting, or cooking.

Looking at the present as a three-second window and remaining focused on what I am doing at this time, has been very useful in managing my anxiety during the pandemic.

Remaining present and focusing on the now has become a new norm for me.

Whether I am working in my capacity as a kindergarten teacher, or developing my public profile for my business, I know that it is essential to remain focused on the now.

As easy as it is for me to say this, it takes a lot of effort to remember to remain present, particularly when challenging situations arise. It is important to acknowledge the difficulty of remaining present, and if you find that you are not present, be kind to yourself.

It seems to me, that a big part of the Australian culture is based around being hard on ourselves for our short comings. However, this is not a good practice to embrace.

KISS OF TAOWAY

During my studies in Holistic Counselling, I learnt that the brain believes whatever we think. Therefore, if we think negatively about ourselves, our brains will believe the negative things we are thinking. It is somewhat similar to the *Universal Law of Attraction;* that which we think, we become.

I prefer to challenge all negative thoughts I have about myself. For example, I was at my work table, cutting wood and fell back against the garage wall cover. Luckily, I did not hurt myself. However, my first thoughts and words were along the lines of, *"Gee, I am clumsy."*

I challenged this thought because I know I am not a clumsy person. This was a simple accident because I was rushing and not concentrating on what I was doing. What I did here was challenge the negative thought about myself and instead focus on the behaviour I was displaying.

On another occasion, I was cutting a wrought iron fence with a grinder and a cutting blade. I was on the last top piece of the fence, and as I cut it, the grinder went through faster than I thought, and I cut my finger. Immediately I put pressure on the wound and rushed inside, calling to my partner, *"Get the Metho!"*

Metho fixes everything, right?!

After cleaning my finger and putting a band aid on it, we lay down on the bed and had a chat. My partner asked me, *"What were you thinking, just before you cut yourself?"*

When I thought about it, I realised my mind was already about four or five steps ahead, thinking about what I had to do down the bottom of the fence to cut the poles off, so I could use them in the vegetable garden.

In this situation, I realise that I had forgotten to remain present, and it could have ended a lot worse. I now remember to remain focused when doing this sort of work.

Initially, I had a lot of fear around contracting Covid-19 whilst working as a Kindergarten Teacher. I was concerned about children still coming to kindergarten unwell, staff being unsure whether they could send the children home. This led to several days off as I had mild cold symptoms. After about three weeks in a row with having sick days, and discussing my concerns with my doctor, I requested to be able to work from home. As it was really close to the end of term, it was suggested to take the rest of the term off on leave.

During the first term holiday, I decided I had to complete my Diploma of Holistic Counselling. Over the school holidays, I completed the last few case studies and submitted the paperwork.

Around the second week of term two was when I found out I had passed all requirements; I was extremely pleased with my achievement and proceeded to promote myself.

In the early days of the pandemic, I offered my services for free to support people who were struggling with the prospects the pandemic was creating.

As I mentioned earlier, I believed that Covid-19 was the Universe's way of making us all stop and re-evaluate our lives.

I have said several times over the last six or seven months that, *"This is our full stop. Our do over time."*

Life as we know it has changed forever.

KISS OF TAOWAY

Lots of people are pushing for things to go back to normal, however Covid-19 has had such an effect that there is no going back.

I remember going to the shops at Keysborough around March or April. The potential impact of Covid-19 was finally impacting me. Unfortunately for my partner and other shoppers, my anxiety showed up in the form of song.

As I got out the car I broke out into a rendition of "*It is The End Of The World*" by R.E.M.

This same response has come several times as I have past the local bottle shop, where I have broken out singing, "*My, my, myyyy Corona!*" at the sight of *Corona* beer in the displays. I am happy to say that since writing this, I have got a handle on this and no longer break out into song about our predicament. Well, that is in public. I still sing what I like whilst I am at home.

Over the last two years, I have done a lot of learning. This has helped me to develop more flexibility. It has been a huge asset for me during the pandemic.

Not only did I complete my course, but I also found myself in a situation where I was able to develop new skills in both my professional and private life.

The flexibility I have developed in the last two years has enabled me to transition into working remotely from home, doing data processing, learning to use *Excel*, and expanding my knowledge of how to use *Microsoft Office*.

Along with this learning, I have developed many abilities and skills. Each day, I continue to learn. After all, isn't that the meaning of life?

The benefits of going online have also meant that I have been able to continue in my *Toastmasters* journey, as well. Learning how to give an effective speech, as well as run meetings online has been a steep learning curve for me.

The increase in the use of online platforms has offered me a lot of opportunities to both practice my speaking skills through *Toastmasters* and meetings with work, as well as my written communication skills. During the first lockdown of the pandemic in Victoria, I put several posts on my business page, in some of the local community groups and in the Covid-19 Centre on *Facebook*, offering free counselling sessions to people who were struggling with the impact the Coronavirus was having on them.

I was able to help a few people, by spending a small amount of time on *Messenger* with them, helping them to understand how they were feeling, accepting it was understandable and also assisting them to come up with some ways to manage how they were feeling moving forward.

Helping those people who reached out to me for a chat gave me a great sense of fulfilment. I was able to help them understand that feeling stressed or anxious because of the pandemic was not unusual and that it was a common thing many people were facing. Working through what they could do in their own homes to help get some sort of control back into their lives was a little challenging as I was not aware of their circumstances, however things I suggested were either welcomed or led these individuals to come up with their own ideas.

KISS OF TAOWAY

Sitting here, writing this, I just realised how far I have come in such a short period of time.

Making a positive impact on the lives of others is a very rewarding thing to do.

I also realised that not only have I been having this positive impact on the world, but I am doing it at home with my family, too.

This is where it all begins.

It reminds me of a saying I came up with some time ago; "*Heal your mind, heal your life.*"

I still believe that. I also believe that all the positive impact you have on the world and individuals means nothing if you are not whole within yourself.

Self-care and self-love are the corner stones of a lot of the learning I have done. There is a great analogy that coaches use when working with individuals or in groups.

"*If the oxygen mask drops down to you, when you are in a plane, whose mask do you put on first? Yours or your child's/partner's/parent's mask?*"

I learnt this in an *EQ Workshop*, as well as from my sister who is a Holistic Life Coach.

If we do not look after ourselves first, then we are not going to be able to be around to help others.

TAO OF FLOW

Looking after your own health and wellbeing; physical, mental, emotional, and spiritual, is the most important thing we can do for ourselves, as well as all those we are of service to.

In closing, Covid-19 has made myself - and everyone else - slow down. I have made a concerted effort to spend time reflecting on who I am and what my goals and aspirations are, taken an inventory of my own health and wellbeing from a holistic perspective, and made sure that I use the extended time at home to develop new and old skills.

This has been a challenging time; however, I am looking forward to the proverbial light at the end of the tunnel and what opportunities the future will hold.

CHAPTER 11

THE KISS OF TAOWAY

The *KISS of Taoway* sums up what I call my KISS principles. I have no doubt that many of you would have heard of the KISS acronym, *"Keep it simple stupid."*

This is a principle I learnt from my Dad and decided I wanted to incorporate this wisdom into my book, as it sums up a lot of my philosophical perspective on life.

However, I have modified this acronym to something that suits my perspective much better. In the original version, the word stupid immediately brings up thoughts of myself or others being stupid or inept, thus I felt that this was the wrong perspective for me to share with the world.

KISS OF TAOWAY

When we are working with the mind and delving deeper into the metaphysical, language is very important. Our minds believe whatever we see, hear, taste, touch, smell, and think. If we think of a big juicy steak or a block of chocolate, many chemical reactions begin to take place in our body in anticipation for this treat.

This same thing occurs when we think about ourselves. If we think negatively about ourselves, our bodies create chemical reactions that create the emotions and feelings that accompany those negative thoughts as it would if someone else had said them or did something to cause that feeling.

On the other hand, if we think positive thoughts about ourselves, our body creates the positive reactions within us that mirror those thoughts and create an outward positive view of who we are.

For this reason, whilst meditating, I came up with my own version of the KISS principle, by changing that one negative word into a positive word. Thus, my *"Keep it Simple Solution"* was born.

I believe that for every problem and obstacle in life, there is always a simple solution that we can follow through with and create a new present and future for ourselves.

After coming up with my *"KISS"* principles, I decided I need to collate them. What I found, was that majority of these principles fit into 1 of 4 different categories.

These four categories are my *MVPA's*, or *Mindset Values Priceless Assets*. These are key ideas or perspectives that I believe are invaluable to me, and I hope are of use to you.

THE KISS OF TAOWAY

In relation to the *"KISS"* principles, *MVPA* stands for:

- ☯ **Mindset**
- ☯ **Values**
- ☯ **Priceless**
- ☯ **Assets**

None of these principles are of more value than the others, however saying that, I do personally believe that addressing your **Mindset** is of utmost importance.

If you find, as many people do throughout their lives, that you have a fixed mindset, then it is possible for you to choose and work towards developing a growth mindset. I am not saying that a fixed mindset is a negative, however it may cause more challenges when you are attempting to make changes in your life.

A fixed mindset may prevent you from getting a new job in any field except that which you have experience in, it may put barriers up against friendships you might otherwise develop, and it may prevent you from learning new skills you are capable of learning.

This can be summarized up by the statement a colleague of mine told me, due to certain issues she was having at work. She said *"I am loud, that's who I am. I've always been loud, and I cannot change that."*

Then she referred to her age. This worried me because I could see that she had the potential to change. I used my own Mother and her growth since my Father died as the opposing argument, telling my colleague, *"You can change if you want to; look at my Mum. Since my Dad passed away, she has learnt how to use the lawnmower to cut the grass, do landscaping, paint rooms and use an electric drill. You just have to be willing to change."*

Some people find it difficult to change. It can be scary because you are going into the unknown. However, it is not as scary as one day looking back on your life and wishing you had done it.

Mindset:

- You must create a growth mindset.
- You need to look at obstacles as opportunities.
- Looking for what you can learn from any given event is essential to being able to manifest synchronicity in your life.
- Be flexible.
- Be prepared to change in light of what has happened.
- Be open to change.
- Have a go.
- Do not be afraid to try something new.
- Expand your horizons.
- Do something you have always wanted to do.

In my experience, it was my mindset that I began to focus on when it felt like my life was tumbling down around me. I also refer to perspectives when referring to mindset. I do not believe I had a fixed mindset before my separation and Father's death. However, I believe that since then, I have nourished my mindset, focusing on potentials rather than deficits that could come from my experiences.

I definitely looked at all the obstacles and stressors I was facing at the time as challenges that I knew I could face and would help me to become the person I am. As I was looking for opportunities to learn, I noticed that I was able to glimpse more synchronicities in life.

Flexibility at times was a challenge, and sometimes is still a challenge I face. Flexibility comes with time, as we learn to push our boundaries past where we feel comfortable and safe, to the new learnings and opportunities that are always there, just out of reach to us in the present moment.

Along with challenging these fixed mindsets and developing a more growth-based mindset, we learn that it is ok to have a go. No one ever fails if they have a go. The worst we do, is learn a way that is not successful. The best is that we learn a new way of doing or being.

Once you have focused on your mindset and have begun to develop the growth mindset I have discussed, you will be more confident and willing to try new things, particularly new things you have always wanted to do.

Values:

- Learn about your values; what they are, what you will accept and what are deal breakers.
- When you can look at obstacles as opportunities, you will gain a greater understanding of who you are. Coming from this place of knowledge of self, you can use your beliefs and values as your guide to assist you to manifest synchronicity in your life.
- Stay true to your values and constantly reflect upon your journey.
- Embed your values into everyday life.
- Explore your beliefs deeply to make sure they truly resonate with you.
- Read a lot on the topic and speak with those who share your beliefs and learn from their experiences.

- Practice your personal beliefs every day, in everything you do.
- Do not preach to others, but rather lead by example.

Values can easily tell you a lot about yourself. The same can be said about beliefs. In this context, I will discuss values and beliefs as one. This was one of the most important self-reflective tools or activities I did with my Counsellor. I really was not sure what my values truly were. I was rediscovering my beliefs in relation to Spiritualism and who I was. However, my values alluded me.

When I reflect back on the discovery of my personal values, the main deal breaker was control. As a kindergarten teacher, we teach the children in a way that encourages autonomy. This is something I had lost in the latter years of my marriage, for various reasons, including my ongoing battle with mental illness.

Once you are able to determine what your values are, it is essential to embed them into your life and reflect upon them regularly. Explore your beliefs as well and if you find that they are in conflict with your values, then consider redefining your beliefs so that they fit with your values, or alternatively, question the validity of your beliefs.

Knowledge really is power when you are reviewing your beliefs.

It is important to make sure that you read, or research far and wide, as well as speak to people with experience in your beliefs. Personal experience can be extremely powerful.

Whatever your belief is, I believe it is vital that you are able to incorporate this into every aspect of your day-to-day living.

THE KISS OF TAOWAY

Equally, I believe it is important to share this through leading by example, rather than through preaching.

Preaching can be an easy trap to fall into when you feel so wholeheartedly about a belief. Many years ago, before I was married, I was deeply involved in my personal spirituality. I felt so strongly about it that I spoke about it all the time.

Unfortunately, one day I was doing this to someone close to me and we almost ended up in a fight, because they felt like I was preaching to them and I would not back off. Luckily, we resolved the issue, and I learned an important lesson the hard way.

If people want to know more about your beliefs, they will come and ask you about it. This is when you can go deeper into the concepts of your beliefs.

Priceless:

- Priceless is about focusing on the present time.
- Focus on the process of what you are doing, rather than the end result.
- You can only affect the end result through remaining focused on the process in the present.
- Practice mindfulness i.e. meditation, mindful breathing, or mandala drawing. Whatever helps you to remain in the present.
- Now is the only time that matters.
- Remember the "present three".
- Live each day as if you are living the life you want to create.

In the early childhood field, staff often say that the *"Process is more important than the result."*

This concept is an important one to remember when we are stuck in the mundanity of life. It is easy for us to reminisce about the past or dream about the future, however this takes us away from the only time that truly matters; the Present Time.

Too often we get caught in the thoughts of what we aim to achieve, that we forget to appreciate what we already have. An example of this comes from a discussion with my Counsellor. I was saying how I was looking forward to when I eventually see my children again. I then referred to how I had believed I was a bad Father in the past. Bronwyn said, *"Look at how far you have come. You have developed your parenting skills, completed the 'Men's Behaviour Change' program and developed an arsenal of coping strategies for when time get tough."*

It is amazing how people can often see more of you than you can see of yourself. In this situation, I had drifted to the future and forgotten to take an audit of what I was doing in the present.

This is where mindfulness training can come in helpful when we are wanting to focus on the Present Time. There are many great apps on the internet and for your wireless devices that can assist with learning mindfulness, however you do not need to spend any money if you do not want to.

The easiest way I remind myself to remain present is to focus on the breath. By mindfully breathing in and out, focusing on as much or as little of the breath as you want, can be a great way to return to the present when anxiety or depression take a hold of you.

I will usually find a comfortable place to sit, close my eyes and just focus on my breath. Breathing in, 2, 3, 4, breathing out, 2, 3, 4. If I feel so inclined, I will then focus my attention on my nostrils and how it feels as the breath enters the nose. Then I might even follow the breath all the way into my lungs, noticing how my ribs move and the expansion of the lung space opening up to accommodate the life-giving air. I might even follow the air on its journey all the way out of me and start all over again.

However, the choice to remain present is a choice only you can make.

Find what works for you and work with it. Spend time each day practicing your personal mindfulness or Present Time activity, so that it becomes part of who you are and how you live your life.

Assets:

- Be brave, be bold.
- There is nothing you cannot do if you really want to do it.
- Acknowledge and believe you are enough.
- Be authentic.
- Invest in yourself; you are your best asset.

Remember, you are your greatest asset.

Many people also invariably underestimate their worth. One thing I have learnt time and time again during my journey, is that *I am enough*.

KISS OF TAOWAY

So, how do you honour your most important asset? Firstly, I believe you need to remember you are only human and with that comes all the pros and cons of being human.

Next, you need to focus on your can-do's, rather than your cannot do's.

Early Childhood has a perspective of working with children from a strength-based position. The belief is that if we focus on a child or a person's strength, they are more likely to be successful in developing the skills related to those strengths.

It has been proven that when we focus on developing our strengths, that we not only improve that specific area of who we are, but we also lift up other aspects of ourselves. For instance, when we look at a child who is really artistic and creative, and we support them to develop this skill, they also develop their fine motor, cognitive, language skills, amongst many others.

This same concept applies to adults, as well. If we focus on the skills we are good at, then this will also help to develop our skills we are more lacking in.

It has also been proven that when we focus on a deficit model of learning, then we may make some improvement in the deficit, however the degree of learning or improvement will not be anywhere near what a strength-based perspective can give you.

If we think of ourselves as adults, how often do we look at our strengths or skills?

Often, when people are asked this question, they struggle to name one strength or positive thing about themselves. On the contrary, if they are asked to name their weaknesses, many would need several pages and still not have enough space.

Focusing on yourself as your greatest asset, goes against most of the social conditioning you will have been exposed to throughout your life.

However, if you truly focus on your strengths and focus your attention on developing them, you will find that your potential is limitless.

Acknowledging your authentic self in everything you do is key to nourishing yourself and embracing the key asset you are. This brings me to another point that society has guided us down the wrong path.

That is loving yourself. When you hear that, you may perceive people who are self-absorbed, narcissistic, and downright obnoxious.

This, however, could not be further from the truth. In order for us to be the best we can for ourselves, as well as those around us, it is essential that we love and respect ourselves.

Putting ourselves first, in order to be of better service to others is not a selfish act. It is a necessary act.

For many of us, taking care of ourselves is a foreign thing. We may eat a well-balanced diet and exercise, but do we allow ourselves the rest and relaxation we require to be at the top of our game?

In many cases, we allow ourselves to become so run down that we begin to struggle just to look after ourselves. We wish to be able to be supportive to others and continue doing this, however we eventually reach a point where we have nothing else to give.

Investing in yourself is vital to your growth as an individual.

It also means that you will have more to offer those around you. Investing time or money - or both - to enable you to develop the skills or interests that support your strengths, purpose, and values, will return more than you outlay.

The satisfaction you will receive from following your passions will drive you to continue to pursue this investment in yourself. Everyone will benefit from your investment in yourself as you are your most important asset.

May your journey be long and inspiring, whilst you strive to discover your future self in the present.

Love and Light,

John Ledgar
Be the change you want to see .

TAO OF YOUR KISS JOURNEY

Now that you have read my story, my legacy, it is now your turn.

You have two choices.

Choice 1 is that you continue your life journey as before. You can put all that you have learned from me on a back shelf and continue to live your own life and follow your own path.

You can choose to put all you have read down as a fantastical journey, stuck in the world of fantasy and face the challenges of life in your own way.

There is nothing wrong with this path; in fact, this is the path I have led for such a long period of my own life. This is a path

KISS OF TAOWAY

I believe we all have to take for a period during our own life's journey.

This path will be rewarding in itself and will lead you onto greatness in your own time.

Choice 2 is that you take the lessons you have learnt through reading my story and look at the learnings in relation to your own life. You can choose to take heed of what I have learnt upon my journey to help guide you quicker and more efficiently towards the life you want to live.

A lesson I have learnt many times over, is that we are stronger when we can learn both from our own experiences and the experiences of those around us.

In some circles this is called finding the *"Ah ha!"* moment.

As an aspiring *Toastmaster*, I have had many of these *"Ah ha!"* moments through listening to speeches of fellow *Toastmasters*.

This crosses over into all other areas of my life, as well. Reading a book, watching a movie, discussing philosophical perspectives with other Early Childhood Teachers, and observing life can bring many *"Ah ha!"* moments to us, if we are open to the messages that are being given to us.

In the following section, there are some ways that you can continue to use the learnings you have discovered in this book. I look forward to hearing from you about how my journey has inspired you and helped you.

TAO OF YOUR KISS JOURNEY

In life, we often become bogged down in what everyone around us is doing and forget that it is our journey that is the most important.

It is time to make yourself a priority, to see a bigger, more beautiful world around you, even in the darkest and most mundane times.

It is time to put your best foot forward and become the light you came here to be.

Be the change you want to see .

THANK YOU

I would like to thank you for sharing this journey with me. It has been a great experience writing this book and the process has been very cathartic. I would also like to thank several people, in particular.

Mum, thank you for always being there for me when I needed you. You and Dad had a big job raising me and guiding me to become the man I am. I am forever grateful for the love you have given me. You have even helped me to rediscover my own self-worth, through all the little jobs you ask me to do. I did not know that I was capable of so much.

Kaylene, you have been my inspiration for this journey. As I once supported you in your journey to become an author, you have supported me in return. We shared a very special moment together at Goulburn. Though the time went quick, I still remember it very clearly. Also, your program was amazing and helped me get a lot of things down that I would not have been able to.

David, you are my bro. You inspire me from your fearlessness. I have loved every moment we have been able to share together, since we reconnected at the start of my journey. You are a level head that I can speak to when things are dire.

Dianne, words cannot express how much I have appreciated having you walk this path with me. You have been an inspiration in the journey you have shared with me. You were my second set of eyes for much of this book, as well as the ear I could chew with all my ideas and concerns. I know I could have written this book without you, but it would not have been as easy.

Grandma, you were my first spiritual teacher, and much of what I have written has stemmed from what you had taught me as I was growing up, as well as when we reconnected at *Forest Lodge Nursing Home*. I would really have loved to have shared this physically with you, however you were taken to God's Garden before I could complete it. R.I.P.

Dad, I often feel you when I am in the garden or by the fire. I am reminded of you when I see the fresh shoots of spring. You were a true legend of your own time. There were many things you taught me, such as mowing the lawn, creating a budget, and putting a bed together. I am forever blessed for the time we spent together, particularly in those last couple of weeks. R.I.P.

To my children, Charlotte, Zoe, and Adam, I am your Father, in the words of Darth Vader. And I will love you until my last breath and beyond. I am very proud of the people you are growing into. May you enjoy this book when the time is right.

To the rest of my family, friends, colleagues, and acquaintances, thank you for all being a part of my journey. Though some of the relationships were difficult, I would not change one thing, for that would change who I am today. Blessings to you all.

ABOUT THE AUTHOR

John Ledgar is the eldest son of David and Lavinia Ledgar. He was born on a Tuesday morning, on the 11th February 1975. John has an older sister, Kaylene and a younger brother, David.

John attended Overport Primary School, followed by Frankston High School, in Frankston South.

After finishing high school, John found himself unemployed, doing a variety of casual manual labour jobs, until he was able to sit the Police entrance exam.

This is the only career John had ever considered; thus, he was heartbroken when he failed the exam. John persisted and researched opportunities to get to his desired goal.

After some time, John enrolled in the Bachelor of Arts at La Trobe University, Bendigo. This was a deep learning experience for John as he struggled with adulthood, responsibility, study, and temptation.

After two years, John transferred to Monash University Clayton where he completed his Bachelor of Arts, majoring in History, and minoring in Politics, Sociology, and Geography.

Again, John found himself unemployed. He eventually began work for the dole at Patterson Lakes Primary School, where he worked for 18 months, which ultimately led to him studying a Graduate Diploma of Early Childhood Education and becoming a kindergarten teacher.

During his career as a kindergarten teacher, John has worked in both long day childcare, and sessional kindergarten. John has served as a Union Representative for the staff at the local council where he currently works for two years; attending Union meetings at the Australian Education Union, rallies and even meetings with state members of Parliament.

John is currently an OHS rep whilst working relief across the local council that employs him.

John has had a lifelong interest in spirituality and the paranormal. He has read extensively on the topic and after his epiphany, is now a trained Holistic Counsellor.

John has been blessed with healing hands, though he understands that he is but a channel for the work of Spirit. To John, Spirit sums up for him, what many people would refer to as God, Allah, Jehovah, or any other name given to their deity.

ABOUT THE AUTHOR

John lives a humble life with his partner, Dianne, two Chihuahuas, Molly and Maggie, two cats, Bella and Gizmo, and fish, Texas, in the South East of Melbourne Victoria, no more than 20 minutes from where he grew up.

John has three children from a previous relationship, that he loves and adores more than anything. John also has been extremely lucky to inherit nine, incredible grandchildren with his partner Dianne, who he also loves and adores.

TAOWAY CONNECTION

Now you have glimpsed into my life, struggles, and victories… What next?

Now is the time for you to reflect upon your own life and see where your struggles are, how you can overcome them and celebrate your victories.

CONNECT WITH ME

If you are just starting off on a life-changing journey, there are many ways you can engage with me, by liking my Facebook page by following the link to my John Ledgar – Spiritual Healer page: https://www.facebook.com/TaoLiong22/

You can also look me up on Instagram by following the link to my page: https://www.instagram.com/kiss_of_taoway/

You can also follow me on LinkedIn by searching for *"John Ledgar Holistic Counsellor."*

SPECIAL OFFERS

For purchasing and reading my book and sharing in the journey of my life, you have access to a couple of eBooks I have created as a special offer for you.

The first book is a simple little read about the benefits of meditation. It also has a guided meditation you can do in your own time.

To receive this special offer, email me at johnledgar1066@gmail.com and mention the special offer word: **KISSofMeditation**.

https://sqribble.net/home

KISS OF TAOWAY

You can also obtain a copy of my *Words of Inspiration* eBook. A stunningly visual eBook full of wisdom I have received both during my darkest hours, as well as during my celebrations in life.

To receive this special offer, email me at johnledgar1066@gmail.com and mention the special offer word: **KISSofInspiration**.

https://sqribble.net/home

If you are interested in both eBooks, use the special offer word: ***KISSspecialOffer.***

MEDITATION GROUP

If you are interested in learning mediation with me, you are welcome to join my Meditation group, which I run once a week. You do not need any skill at meditation, just an openness and willingness to learn. Alternatively, you can book private sessions for one-on-one tutelage in meditation.

HOLISTIC COUNSELLING

As a Holistic Counsellor, I am trained to work with you, to help you to resolve issues and concerns in your life. Using a variety of both counselling and holistic tools, we can delve into your life and help you to find the solutions to what is happening. Counselling is available for a range of challenges in life including:

- Relaxation and Stress Counselling
- Life Skills Counselling
- Social Relationship Counselling
- Self-Esteem and Motivational Counselling

Along with the focuses above, you may want to explore holistic tools such as:

- Meditation, Mindfulness and Relaxation therapy
- Tarot Cards
- Spirit Guides
- Regression Therapy
- Colour Therapy

KISS OF TAOWAY

- ☯ Art Therapy
- ☯ Sound Therapy
- ☯ Dream Therapy

Together we can explore the depth of your psyche and untap your full potential.

The best thing about Holistic Counselling, is you do not have to have any problems to receive the benefits. Holistic Counselling can assist you to gain a deeper insight to your own potential and help you clarify your goals.

You will explore your values and look at your life through a fresh lens. It is only through looking critically at ourselves, with a loving heart, that we can bring about the positive changes we wish to make in our lives.

You will discover the Tarot as a great resource for self-exploration, as well as using sound and music in your own exploration. Regression can be very interesting experience and you will enjoy being guided through this experience. You will also explore meditation, mindfulness, and relaxation.

You will embark on this journey independently with me as your guide, until you are prepared to explore your path alone.

As a special offer, you can receive discounted rates on my Holistic Counselling sessions. For 1-2 sessions, you will receive a 30% discount, 3-4 sessions you will receive a 40% discount, and 5 or more sessions, you will receive a 50% discount when you book, using the special offer word: **KISSofHolisticCounselling**.

This offer is only available once per person.

PELLOWAH

"Pellowah is a beautiful modality that will assist you to gain greater insight into life. Pellowah is an angelic word that means "Radical Shift in Consciousness." It was created by Kachina Ma'an in 2003. Pellowah connects the 12 strands of DNA ready for activation. It also unblocks and realigns all the meridians and chakras within the body." (Pellowah Melbourne)

A Pellowah session generally goes for around 45 minutes to an hour, however I suggest that you put aside at least 1 and a half hour of time to ensure you get the most benefit from the experience.

What people can experience during a Pellowah sessions are things like:

- Colours in front of their eyes
- Visions
- Sounds

KISS OF TAOWAY

- ☯ Smells
- ☯ Feeling of contentment

Some people, such as me, have a sense of calm which stays with them for days, followed by a shift in their consciousness. They begin to think on a different level, much deeper and more universal.

As a special offer, you can receive discounted rates on Pellowah sessions. For 1-2 sessions, you will receive a 30% discount, 3-4 sessions you will receive a 40% discount, and 5 or more sessions, you will receive a 50% discount when you book using the special offer word: **KISSofPellowah**.

This offer is only available once per person.

SPIRITUAL HEALING

Spiritual healing is something that I have been blessed with. Often called the *"laying on of hands,"* a term I learnt at the Victorian Spiritualist Union whilst I undertook the *"Spiritualism Training Course"* in 2019. Spiritual healing is when a person channels the healing energy of spirit through them to a recipient. Spiritual healing can be done on anyone and anything.

I have had many pleased clients both personally and working as a Spiritual Healer at Mornington and Seaford Spiritualist Churches, respectively. I have also participated in healing sessions at the Berwick Spiritualist Church.

Conducting spiritual healing is very special to me, as it allows me to assist others to work through their problems from an energetic level.

Spiritual healing was extremely comforting during the period my Father was in hospital and whilst he was passing from this world. It gave me the strength to support my Father, Mother, brother, and sister at the most painful time in our lives.

It has also helped me to shift some of the feelings and emotions around my separation and more importantly, my separation from my children.

As a special offer I am going to give you a complimentary Spiritual Healing Session, to experience the gift I have been blessed with.

Book using the special offer word: **KISSofHealing**.

This offer is only available once per person.

THE "BE THE CHANGE YOU WANT TO SEE" PROGRAM

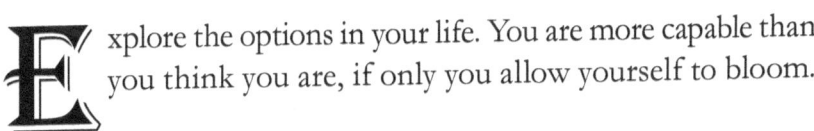

Explore the options in your life. You are more capable than you think you are, if only you allow yourself to bloom.

In the *"Be The Change You Want To See"* program, you will explore your values, beliefs, interests, and passions and put them together into a purpose-built vehicle for the future you are blessed to live.

You will explore:

- ☯ Your life as a whole, discovering what is most important to you.
- ☯ Learn to set realistic and effective goals.

- ☯ Discover your values and how to determine them and work with them.
- ☯ Share your interests and how you can use these to live a more meaningful life. What drives you and gives life meaning to you and how to incorporate this into all aspects of your life.
- ☯ Learn about synchronicity and how to use this to empower your life.
- ☯ Discover simple mindfulness activities and how they can help you to remain present to get the fullest out of your life.
- ☯ Discover your personality and how it impacts on you day to day.
- ☯ Learn about control dramas.

Do not wait until life has you pinned under a rock to explore your potential. Join me for an intensive look at yourself and design the life you were born to live. For bookings, use the special offer word: **KISSofLife**.

One-on-one and small group options available.

John Ledgar HH Dip (H.C.)
Spiritual Healer
Holistic Counsellor
Spiritual Guide
0417801201
John Ledgar-Spiritual Healer
Connect:fb.me/TaoLiong22
m.me/TaoLiong22
johnledgar1066@gmail.com
ABN:93696572601

NOTES

KISS OF TAOWAY

NOTES

www.ingramcontent.com/pod-product-compliance
Lightning Source LLC
Chambersburg PA
CBHW021150080526
44588CB00008B/286